D1139442

GREAT BRITISH FOOD REVIVAL

MICHEL ROUX JR. ✤ ANGELA HARTNETT

GREGG WALLACE ✤ CLARISSA DICKSON WRIGHT

THE HAIRY BIKERS ✤ MATT TEBBUTT

GARY RHODES ✤ JAMES MARTIN

AINSLEY HARRIOTT ✤ GLYNN PURNELL

and

BLANCHE VAUGHAN

First published in hardback in Great Britain in 2011 by

Weidenfeld & Nicolson, an imprint of the Orion Publishing Group Ltd

Orion House, 5 Upper St Martin's Lane, London WC2H 9EA

an Hachette UK Company

1 3 5 7 9 10 8 6 4 2

© Outline Productions 2011

© Blanche Vaughan 2011 p15, p16, p18, p19, p20, p21, p35, p38, p39, p40, p43, p44, p45, p56, p59, p60, p62, p63, p65, p78, p79, p80, p81, p84, p85, p87, p100, p101, p103, p104, p105, p107, p118, p120, p121, p123, p124, p125, p126, p138, p139, p142, p143, p145, p146, p147, p161, p162, p163, p165, p166, p168, p169, p180, p182, p183, p186, p189, p190, p191, p202, p205, p206, p207, p211, p212, p213

© Michel Roux Jr. p11, p12, p15; Angela Hartnett p30, p33, p34; Gregg Wallace p50, p52, p55; Clarissa Dickson Wright p71, p72, p75; The Hairy Bikers p92, p95, p96; Matt Tebbutt p112, p114, p117; Gary Rhodes p133, p134, p137; James Martin p152, p155, p156–57; Ainsley Harriott p174, p176–77, p179; Glynn Purnell p199, p200, p203

Contributors: Sam Hart, Eddie Hart and Nieves Barragan of Barrafina, London p37; Jim Sutcliffe of Meridian Meats p76; © Yotam Ottolenghi ((This recipe is extracted from *Ottolenghi: The Cookbook* by Yotam Ottolenghi and Sami Tamimi, (Ebury Press, 2008)) p98; The Hamill family of The Hive Honey Shop p190

All rights reserved. No part of this publication may be reproduced, stored in a retrieval system, or transmitted, in any form or by any means, electronic, mechanical, photocopying, recording or otherwise, without the prior permission of both the copyright owner and the above publisher.

A CIP catalogue record for this book is available from the British Library.

Photography by Andrew Hayes-Watkins

Design & Art Direction by Kate Barr

Art Editor Natasha Webber

Editorial: Amanda Harris, Nicola Crossley, Diona Murray & Constance Novis and Cherry Ekins

978 0 297 86514 8

Printed and bound in Germany

The Orion Publishing Group's policy is to use papers that are natural, renewable and recyclable and made from wood grown in sustainable forests. The logging and manufacturing processes are expected to conform to environmental regulations of the country of origin.

www.orionbooks.co.uk

CONTENTS

WOLVERHAMPTON PUBLIC LIBRARIES	
XB000000099145	
Bertrams	08/04/2011
641.5941GR	£20.00
F	01264586

INTRODUCTION

The best of British food is truly delicious. This book is a celebration – and a reminder – of the enormous range of local varieties and different breeds that make up our food heritage.

It is also timely, because home-grown food is under threat as never before. Food fashions, convenience foods and competition from cheaper foreign imports have changed what is grown and produced – and therefore what we eat – and local, seasonal food in all its variety is finding it tough to survive.

But Britain's larder has so much to offer that the best chefs in the country have joined forces to champion the best of home-grown food.

In this cookbook, Michel Roux Jr. celebrates our bread-making skills, Angela Hartnett discovers the riches of local crab, Gregg Wallace shares his devotion to British potatoes, Clarissa Dickson Wright declares her love for the British Lop, Gary Rhodes finds the smell and taste of home-grown tomatoes irresistible, the Hairy Bikers enjoy the versatility of the Lincoln cauliflower, Mark Tebbutt revisits the almost-forgotten glories of mutton, James Martin creates deliciously fresh apple dishes, Ainsley Harriott presents the case for how tasty our wild honey truly is and Glynn Purnell delves into local cheese delights.

Melton Mowbray pork pies, Cornish potted crab, Herefordshire apple crumbles and Lancashire cheese and chutney sandwiches – it would be a travesty if they were reduced to being made with imported produce. National and regional specialities should be demanded from our supermarkets and bought at farmer's markets. They should be sought out, celebrated, and most importantly, eaten.

The famous chefs who have initiated this call to arms are convinced there is nothing better than to enjoy the delicious taste of home-grown food produced at the peak of its season and these delicious recipes will help you share their passion.

BREAD

BREAD
with RECIPES *by* MICHEL ROUX JR.

Gone are the days when a trip to the bakery was part of the daily routine. Once, the sight of hot loaves being shovelled out of a great oven by flour-dusted bakers, and the enticing smell of freshly baked bread wrapped in brown paper to take home warm, was as usual as buying the newspaper.

All too often these days, pre-packaged, mass-produced loaves have become our daily bread. As the bread-making process has become more and more industrialised, Britain has gone from having 30,000 high-street bakers in the 1950s to fewer than 4,000 today. As many as nine million loaves are purchased in the UK every day but an artisan baker produces only a miniscule percentage of that total.

Real bread is food for the soul. A true baker will tell you that the best tools he has are his own two hands. Authentic artisan bread contains only four ingredients: flour, water, yeast and salt. It has a completely different texture and flavour to mass-produced loaves baked according to the Chorley Wood Bread Process. This was introduced in the 1960s, and it enables dough to be heated quickly to reduce production time. There are obviously cost-related benefits here but they come at a price: salt and yeast contents are higher in bread made using this process, and numerous synthetic ingredients and vegetable fats are added. Bread like this may have a place in the market but a staggering 80% of our bread is made this way.

Great breads have a variety of wonderful flavours and textures, and each loaf has been created for a purpose. From chewy sourdough to rich dark rye, crunchy granary to a light soft bun, the options are many. A nutty, dark loaf can be an ideal companion to cheese, or a buttery, sweet white can be used to make a delicious dessert. It's time we all understood and respected the dedication of the true artisan baker who sticks to the traditional methods, taking time and care to bring us this humble yet proud and complex product.

Thankfully there are signs that a bread revival is under way. Artisan bakers are returning to the high-street and diversifying to meet modern demands. Some deliver bread to your door while others supply local cafes, restaurants and farmers' markets. If you aren't lucky enough to have such bakers near you, here are delicious yet simple bread recipes to try in your own kitchen.

SANDWICH BREAD LOAF

This is an easy-to-make alternative to white sliced bread. The milk and butter in the recipe make it rich, but it is not as fatty as a brioche. Delicious and versatile, it is a great bread to have in the fridge as it keeps well. I prefer to cook it as a loaf in a tin, but it is equally good shaped into little individual buns. The recipe is made with white flour but also works well with a mix of brown, rye or wholemeal flour, though the end result will be a little heavier. It is also great with a few sultanas and cumin seeds, to serve with cheese. *Michel Roux Jr.*

Serves 6
- 10g dried yeast
- 350ml milk, warmed
- 250g plain white flour
- 250g strong white bread flour
- 20g golden syrup
- 10g sea salt
- 25g melted butter

You will need a 12 x 20cm loaf tin.

Dissolve the yeast in the warm milk in a large bowl. Then add all the other ingredients. Stir until well mixed and lump free, cover and leave for 5 minutes.

Turn out on a lightly floured surface. Knead the dough for 10 minutes until smooth and elastic. Return the dough to the bowl, cover and leave in a warm, draft-free place to ferment and rise for at least an hour or until almost doubled.

When the dough has nearly doubled in size, preheat the oven to 220°C/425°F/Gas 7. Grease and flour the loaf tin and set aside. Knock the dough back and shape it into two equal-sized balls. Place these into the bread tin side-by-side, cover and leave to rise again.

When the dough has risen to the top of the tin, slash the surface using a razor blade or a very sharp knife and immediately place in the oven. After 10 minutes turn the oven down to 180°C/350°F/Gas 4 and bake for 30 minutes. When the bread is golden brown on top, tip out of the tin and leave to cool on a wire rack.

BREAD CHARLOTTE
with CONFIT DUCK

This is a great family dish, a Roux household favourite for festivities, especially at Christmas. The duck confit, along with the gizzards, can be purchased in most supermarkets or good delis. If you are squeamish then omit the hearts or replace them with a few duck livers. The recipe is for four people but you can multiply it up for a large table of 10 or 12. Use a spring form cake tin – it looks great brought to the table and piled high with wild mushrooms. Lovely with a good glass of Côtes du Rhône red or a Barolo, this dish can be cooked well in advance and kept warm for an hour before serving. Perfect for a lazy lunch. *Michel Roux Jr.*

Serves 4

Duck
2 confit duck legs,
    fat drained and reserved
2 confit gizzards,
    or a few duck livers, sliced
2 confit hearts

Charlotte
½ loaf good-quality white bread
duck fat, from the confit

Sauce
3 shallots, chopped
duck fat, from the confit
200ml port
600ml veal stock

Mushrooms
duck fat, from the confit
200g mixed wild mushrooms, trimmed
2 garlic cloves, chopped
2 tbsp parsley, chopped
freshly ground black pepper
wild mushrooms, to serve

Preheat the oven to 180°C/350°F/Gas 4. Cut the bread into medium-thick slices. Remove the crust then cut the slices in half again. Moisten the slices with some of the duck fat. Line the springform cake tin or pudding basin with the bread, making sure the slices overlap and are pressed well into the sides.

Sweat the shallots in a pan with a little duck fat then add the port and reduce by half. Add the stock and reduce until syrupy. Remove from the heat and leave to cool. Put some duck fat into another frying pan and add the mushrooms to sear. Add the chopped garlic and parsley, cook for only a few minutes and then set aside to cool.

Remove the skin from the duck legs and flake the meat into a large bowl. Add the sliced gizzards and hearts (or duck livers, if using). Add to this the mushrooms and just enough of the sticky sauce to bind, and season generously with ground black pepper. Pack this mixture into the bread-lined dish. Cover the top with a piece of foil and bake for 35–40 minutes. Leave to rest for 10 minutes before taking out of the tin. Serve with the remaining port sauce and a few extra sautéed wild mushrooms.

DIPLOMAT PUDDING

This was the first dessert that I learnt to make as an apprentice. I was a 16-year-old trainee chef in Paris. This simple yet delicious French version of bread and butter pudding is very special to me. It can be made as individual puddings or in a terrine and then sliced. Best to eat at room temperature and not fridge cold, otherwise the delicate rum and vanilla flavours will be lost. The bread used can be a mixture of whatever you have to hand but should always be toasted in the oven with a dusting of icing sugar. *Michel Roux Jr.*

Serves 6

Pudding
4 slices of good-quality loaf
    bread, crusts removed
icing sugar, for dusting
2 tbsp golden raisins
2 tbsp sultanas
60ml dark rum
apricot jam, warmed, to glaze

Crème anglaise
250ml milk
250ml single cream
150g caster sugar
4 free-range eggs
1 vanilla pod, seeds scraped out
butter, for greasing

You will need 6 small ramekins and a bain-marie.

Cut all the bread into large dice, and spread evenly on a baking sheet. Dust with a little icing sugar and toast in a moderate oven, until crisp. Remove and set the oven to 140°C/285°F/Gas 2. Place the raisins and sultanas in a pan and cover with cold water, bring to a boil then strain into a dish. Add the rum and leave to cool.

For the crème anglaise, mix the milk, cream, sugar and eggs together in a large bowl then pass through a sieve. Stir in the vanilla seeds and set aside. Butter 6 individual-sized ramekin dishes and 6 pieces of foil large enough to cover each dish.

Stir the bread pieces into the raisin, sultana and rum mixture and divide between the ramekin dishes. Ladle the milk mixture over the bread in each dish. Cover with the buttered foil and place into a bain-marie.

Bake for 30 minutes or until set. Set on a wire rack to cool and then refrigerate. To serve, turn out of the dishes and glaze with a little warmed apricot jam.

ANCHOVY TOAST

Serves 6   12 very thin slices of sandwich bread
1 tin of anchovies, in oil
30g butter, softened
freshly ground black pepper

Preheat the grill. Lightly grill both sides of the bread until it is just starting to brown. Drain the anchovies, mash together with the butter and season well with black pepper. Spread the paste over half of the slices of the toasted bread then lay the remaining slices over top.

Using a large board or flat plate, press on the sandwiched toast slices firmly to squash the top and bottom pieces together.

Finally, carefully remove the crusts and cut into fingers to serve.

BAKED EGGS

Serves 6   30g butter
6 free range eggs
50ml single cream
nutmeg, grated
salt and freshly ground pepper

You will need 6 small ramekins and a roasting tin to use as a bain-marie.

Preheat the oven to 200°C/400°F/Gas 6. Divide the butter into 6 little pieces and put one piece at the bottom of each ramekin. Crack an egg into each one. Pour over a little cream and grate over some nutmeg to season along with some salt and pepper.

Put the ramekins into the roasting tin and pour water around them so that it comes halfway up the sides. Bake in the oven for 10 minutes or until the eggs are still a little wobbly but the white is cooked. Remove carefully and serve immediately with the slices of anchovy toast.

CLASSIC ROAST CHICKEN
with BREAD SAUCE

Serves 4

1.5 kg free range chicken
salt
freshly ground black pepper
lemon, cut in ½
head of garlic, skin on
4–5 sprigs of thyme
2 tbsp olive oil

Bread sauce
10 cloves
570ml full fat milk
small white onion
nutmeg, grated
2 bay leaves
10 black peppercorns
5 juniper berries, bruised
salt and pepper
30g butter
120g white breadcrumbs

Preheat the oven to 200°C/400°F/Gas 6. Remove the chicken from the fridge at least 20 minutes before cooking. Season the inside of the cavity with salt and pepper and push in the lemon halves, the garlic and the thyme. Massage the olive oil into the outside of the bird and sprinkle with more salt and pepper.

Lay the bird in the roasting tray, breast-side down and roast for 40 minutes. Then turn the bird onto its back and roast for a further 30 minutes until the skin is golden, or until the bird is cooked through. Allow it to rest for 15 minutes before carving.

The bread sauce
Pour the milk into a saucepan. Stud the cloves into the onion and add to the pan with a grating of nutmeg. Add the bay leaves, peppercorns, juniper and a pinch of salt. Warm to a simmer then remove from the heat, cover and leave to infuse for at least 30 minutes.

When you are ready to make the bread sauce, take the onion out and then strain the milk through a sieve into a bowl to remove the bay and the rest of the spices.

In a clean saucepan, melt the butter then add the strained milk and breadcrumbs. Cook, stirring for a few minutes or until the breadcrumbs absorb all the milk and swell to make a thick sauce. Season to taste with some salt and pepper.

TUSCAN BREAD SOUP

Serves 6–8   2 tbsp olive oil
200g carrots, peeled and diced
1 red onion, finely diced
3 sticks celery, finely diced
salt and black pepper
3 garlic cloves, sliced
small bunch of parsley, roughly chopped
3–4 sprigs of marjoram, roughly chopped
200g tin of tomatoes, chopped
200g cavolo nero, tough stalks removed, leaves roughly chopped
350g cooked borlotti beans
250g stale sourdough or ciabatta bread, crusts removed
extra virgin olive oil, to serve

In a large, heavy-bottomed saucepan, heat the olive oil. Add the carrots, onion, celery and a good pinch of salt and cook gently for about 5 minutes or until they are soft and just beginning to colour. Add the garlic and continue to cook for a couple of minutes.

Turn up the heat a little and add the herbs and fry briefly. Pour in the tomatoes and stir well. Turn down the heat and continue to cook for another 5 minutes or until the tomatoes are well reduced and you have a thick base of sweet, browned vegetables and tomato.

Add the cavolo nero and cover with about 1 litre of water. Season with salt and pepper and bring to the boil. Then turn down to a simmer and cook for about 5 minutes.

Pour in half of the borlotti beans. Purée the remaining beans with a ladle of the soup liquid, then add to the soup and stir well. Now tear the bread into chunks and place it on the top of the soup, pushing it down slightly with a spoon so that it starts to absorb the liquid. Turn off the heat and leave for about 10 minutes for the bread to become soft. Finally, stir the bread through the soup, check the seasoning and reheat slightly before serving. Serve with a good glug of extra virgin olive oil poured over each bowl.

PIZZA DOUGH *and* TOPPINGS

Makes 4
pizza bases

7g packet dried yeast
150ml warm water
200g flour, plus extra for dusting
200g strong white flour
½ tsp salt
3 tbsp olive oil

Dissolve the yeast in 50ml of the warm water and set aside for 5 minutes to froth up. Sift the flours into a large bowl and add the salt. Make a well in the middle and pour in the yeast, olive oil and the rest of the warm water. Using one hand like a claw and holding the bowl with the other, bring the mixture together so that it forms a wet dough.

Flour a work surface and knead the dough on it for at least 5 minutes or until it becomes smooth and elastic. Put it into an oiled bowl, dust with a little flour, cover loosely with a damp tea towel and leave in a warm place for about 1 hour or until it has doubled in size.

When it has risen sufficiently, give it a couple of gentle kneads to knock it back. Then separate it into 4 balls that fit in the palm of your hand. You can now leave the dough covered, in the fridge until you want to use it. (It will keep well until the next day.)

When you are ready, roll out the balls into thin discs and dust with some more flour. Then leave them to rest for 20 minutes or so while you prepare the toppings. To cook the pizzas, place on a preheated baking sheet or pizza stone and cook in an oven preheated to 240°C/475°F/Gas 9 for about 4–6 minutes.

SWISS CHARD *with* BLACK OLIVES *and* RICOTTA

Makes 4
pizzas

1kg Swiss chard, stalks removed
250g ricotta cheese, crumbled
100g Parmesan cheese, grated

100g black olives, pitted
salt and black pepper
extra virgin olive oil, to serve

Cut the chard stalks into 2cm slices and cook for 3 minutes in boiling, salted water. After 2 minutes, add the chard leaves and cook together for the final minute. Drain and squeeze out as much water as possible. Spread a layer of chard over the pizza base, dot with spoonfuls of ricotta cheese and sprinkle with the Parmesan cheese and the olives. Season well with salt and pepper and bake. Remove and pour over some olive oil to serve.

TOMATO *with* ANCHOVY, CHILLI *and* MOZZARELLA

Makes 4
pizzas

1 tbsp olive oil
2 garlic cloves, sliced
8 salted anchovies
400g tin chopped tomatoes
¼ tsp dried chilli flakes

salt and pepper
2 balls of mozzarella,
  torn into small pieces
basil leaves, torn

Heat the oil in a pan and fry the garlic until just beginning to colour. Add the anchovies and cook for a minute to allow them to melt into the oil. Add the tomatoes and chilli flakes and season well. Cook for 10 minutes or so or until you have a thick sauce.

Spread the tomato sauce thinly on the pizza base. Sprinkle the mozzarella pieces evenly around the base. Bake until the crust forms and the mozzarella has melted. Remove and serve with basil leaves scattered over the top.

RAW TOMATO, ROCKET *and* SHAVED PECORINO

Makes 4
pizzas

extra virgin olive oil
salt and pepper
400g ripe tomatoes,
  cut into small cubes

200g rocket
200g Pecorino cheese, shaved
extra virgin olive oil, to serve

Sprinkle a little olive oil and salt on the base of each pizza and bake 4–6 minutes. When it is cooked, spread the cut tomatoes on top and season well. Sprinkle all over with the rocket and shaved Pecorino. Pour over some more olive oil to serve.

"we include the smell of freshly baked bread absolutely free"

IRISH SODA BREAD

Makes   450g plain flour
1 loaf   1½ tsp bicarbonate of soda
             ½ tsp salt
             2 tsp caster sugar
             60g butter, diced
             400ml buttermilk

Preheat the oven to 220°C/425°F/Gas 7. Sift the flour into a bowl and stir in the bicarbonate of soda, salt and sugar. Using your fingertips, rub the butter into the flour mixture. Make a well in the centre of the flour and pour in the buttermilk.

Using one hand like a claw and the other holding the bowl, stir the flour gradually into the buttermilk until the mixture comes together to form dough. Add a little more buttermilk or water if it is too dry. When the mixture has come together, turn it out onto a floured surface and form into a ball. There is no need to knead the dough for long, in fact, it's best to avoid working it too much as it will become tough and heavy.

Form the dough into a round shape, place on a baking sheet and bake for 35 minutes or until the base sounds hollow when tapped.

SUMMER PUDDING

Serves 6–8   250g blackcurrants, stalks removed
250g redcurrants, stalks removed
100g white currants, stalks removed
1 vanilla pod, seeds scraped out
180g caster sugar
350g raspberries
juice of ½ lemon
500g sliced white sandwich loaf, crusts removed

You will need a bowl or pudding basin of approximately 1.5 litre capacity.

Place all the currants, vanilla seeds and sugar in a large saucepan and heat gently. After a couple of minutes, the currants will start to burst and become juicy. Remove from the heat and add the raspberries and lemon juice and set aside.

Line your pudding bowl with the sliced bread: use a slice for the bottom and then overlap slices around the sides. (It is important to overlap the slices so no fruit can leak out.) Keep back enough slices to cover the top of the pudding.

Pour the cooked fruit into a sieve over a large bowl. Carefully spoon the fruit mixture from the sieve into the lined pudding bowl then pour most of the strained liquid over the top. Place the reserved slices on top to cover and pour over the last of the liquid to soak into the bread.

Cover loosely with Cling film, and then with a plate that fits just inside the rim of the bowl. Set the bowl inside a larger bowl or on a tray with sides in case any liquid spills out and press down the plate with a heavy weight. You could use 3 or 4 full tins or even a heavy pestle and mortar if you have one. Leave for up to 12 hours in the fridge.

When you are ready to serve it, remove the weights, the plate and the Cling film. Slide a knife between the pudding and the inside of the bowl. Put a large serving plate upside down on the top of the bowl. Carefully turn the bowl, and the plate, over together so that the pudding slips out of the bowl onto the upturned plate for serving.

CRAB

CRAB
with RECIPES *by* ANGELA HARTNETT

With its rich fresh white meat and creamy intense dark meat, crab is the most delicate and delicious British shellfish available. Delectable dishes range from simple dressed crab accompanied by rich, lemony mayonnaise and a crisp green salad, to the exotic, complex flavours of spiced crab curry.

More than half the crab caught off the British coast is exported to countries on the continent, particularly France and Spain. The reason for the low demand in the UK can be found in crab's rather old-fashioned image and the widespread belief that it is an expensive and difficult ingredient to prepare and cook. With a new wave of suppliers selling fresh crab prepared and ready for use, there is no reason why we shouldn't rediscover this native food treasure and celebrate our local seafood star.

There are several delicious varieties of crab, with brown crab and spider crab being the most widely available. You can choose to get fully involved with picking and preparing whole fresh crabs – messy and fun and very rewarding – or buy fresh crabmeat that can be prepared simply to create an elegant dish. Fresh crab may be more expensive than some fish, but with its richness and depth of flavour, a little crab goes a long way.

SPIDER CRAB GRATIN

This is a great dinner party dish that will wow your guests just because you are serving it in its own shell. It is so easy to prepare and finish, just multiply the recipe for the number of guests you are expecting, and you'll be making it all the time. Make sure you keep the shells for the next time you make crab bisque. *Angela Hartnett*

Serves 1

1 spider crab, cooked and cooled

Filling
glug of olive oil
½ leek, sliced
1 shallot, finely chopped
1 celery stick, trimmed and sliced
1 tbsp tomato purée
1 tsp root ginger, chopped

2 tsp Dijon mustard
25ml white wine
splash of brandy
dash of hot sauce
zest of 1 lemon
1 tbsp basil, chopped
25g breadcrumbs
25g Gruyère cheese, grated
25g Parmesan cheese, grated

Dismantle the spider crab. Remove the meat from the legs and place in the fridge. Wash and dry the main shell and set it aside until serving.

In a hot pan, add the olive oil. Add the leek, shallot and celery and sauté until soft but not coloured. Add the crabmeat, tomato purée, ginger and Dijon mustard and sauté for 1 minute, stirring to make sure the mix doesn't catch on the pan. Add the white wine and brandy and allow them to reduce. Remove from the pan and add a dash of hot sauce, lemon zest and basil.

Spoon the filling into the shell and cover with a light sprinkle of breadcrumbs, and the Gruyère and Parmesan cheeses and place under the grill for 1–2 minutes before serving.

CRAB CAKES

If you need to make something in a hurry, this is a fantastic dish. The crab cakes can be prepared the day before and left in the fridge overnight. They are a lovely starter you can serve with a chilli salsa or sweet chilli jam and crisp green salad dressed with olive oil, salt and freshly ground black pepper. Create your own interpretation of this dish or simply let the crab speak for itself. *Angela Hartnett*

Serves 3   250g white crabmeat
2 spring onions, finely sliced
1 tbsp coriander, roughly chopped
1 small finger root ginger, peeled
2 red chillies, deseeded
2 free range eggs, 1 for the crab mixture and 1 for the egg wash
1 tbsp water
4 tbsp breadcrumbs
plain flour, for coating
25ml olive oil

Place the crabmeat, spring onion, and coriander in a bowl and stir gently. Whiz the ginger and chilli in a food processor until finely chopped and stir into the crabmeat mixture.

Add enough egg to make the mixture stick together without being too wet. Then stir in the breadcrumbs. Mould the mixture into six evenly sized cakes and place them on a dish. Leave in the fridge for 20 minutes (or overnight) to set.

When you are ready to cook the crab cakes, preheat the oven to 180°C/350°F/Gas 4. Beat the remaining egg with a tablespoon of water. Place the flour, beaten egg wash and breadcrumbs in three seperate dishes. Remove the crab cakes from the fridge and coat in the flour, then dip in the egg wash and then finally coat with the breadcrumbs. Give them a gentle shake to remove any excess.

In a hot frying pan add olive oil. Add the crab cakes and fry for a couple of minutes each side until golden brown. Place crab cakes onto a baking tray. Place in the oven and bake for 5–10 minutes, until they are hot in the centre.

CRAB LINGUINE

One of the freshest and most delicious fish dishes you can have. The white crabmeat, chilli and garlic make a perfect combination. You can spice it up as you require and finish with basil and flat-leaf parsley. *Angela Hartnett*

Serves 4   900g brown crab, cooked
25g sea salt
315g dried linguine

Sauce
55ml olive oil
1 garlic clove, finely chopped
4 spring onions, finely chopped
½ tsp fresh red chilli, finely chopped
275g picked fresh white crabmeat
25ml dry white wine
1 tbsp flat-leaf parsley, chopped
1 tbsp basil, chopped
salt and pepper

Dismantle the brown crab by removing the undercarriage. Discard the 'dead man's fingers' and any white meat within the main shell. Put the brown crabmeat aside to be frozen, this can be used to make Crab on Toast (p 37). Then crack the two large front claws: this is where the majority of the delicious white crabmeat will be. Set on a metal tray and check for any shell by scraping the crabmeat along the tray. Place in the fridge.

Bring a large pan of water to the boil, add sea salt and cook the linguine for 7–8 minutes, or according to packets instructions.

Meanwhile, heat the olive oil in a large, deep frying pan and add the garlic, spring onions and chilli. Fry lightly without colouring for one minute. Stir in the white crabmeat and heat through for another minute. Add the wine to the pan and allow it to bubble and reduce completely.

When the linguine is cooked al dente, drain it and add to the crab mixture. Stir in the parsley and basil, and toss everything together to coat evenly. Season to taste and serve immediately.

CRAB *on* TOAST

Similar to the Basque dish known as Txangurro, this makes an excellent light lunch at home. Or, for a picnic, take the crab mix in a bowl with the toast wrapped up separately. You can buy picked crabmeat at all good fishmongers but cooking and picking the crab yourself will not only yield better results, it will be considerably cheaper. Just buy a large, live crab and cook it in boiling salty water for about 25 minutes. Leave to cool before picking the meat.

Serves 4

Crab

70ml olive oil

2 leeks, finely diced

4 shallots, very finely diced

2 garlic cloves, finely
   sliced lengthways

3 bay leaves

100ml crab bisque

20ml tomato purée

¼ tsp cayenne pepper

250g white crabmeat

20-40g brown crabmeat

salt and pepper

4 thick slices of white sourdough bread

1 garlic clove, peeled

Salad

2 heads of red chicory, leaves separated

7 breakfast radishes, sliced lengthways
   on a mandolin

bulb of fennel, finely sliced

Pink Lady apple, sliced into
   half-moon shapes

1 tbsp tarragon, finely chopped

80ml extra virgin olive oil

40ml Moscatel vinegar

In a large frying pan heat the olive oil and fry the leeks, shallots, sliced garlic and bay leaves until translucent, about 7 minutes. Add the bisque, tomato purée and cayenne pepper, and bring to the boil. Reduce by two-thirds.

Stir in the crabmeat, season well with salt and pepper and cook for 2 more minutes. Remove from the heat and transfer to a bowl. Cover with Cling film and leave to cool in the fridge for 2–3 hours.

Half an hour before you are ready to serve, place the chicory, radish, fennel and apple into a large salad bowl. In a smaller bowl, whisk together the olive oil, vinegar and a little salt and pepper and set aside.

Lightly toast the bread. Rub the upper side of the toast with the garlic. To serve, spoon the crab evenly over the toast. Give the dressing another whisk, dress the salad and serve it with the crab toasts.

CRAB *and* SWEETCORN SOUP

Serves 4   4 cobs of sweetcorn or 700g tinned sweetcorn, drained
½ tsp salt and pepper
1 tbsp sesame oil
100g spring onions, finely sliced plus a little extra, to serve
10g root ginger, peeled and grated
1 red chilli, deseeded and finely chopped
1 tbsp dry sherry or Chinese rice wine
200g fresh white crabmeat
1 tbsp cornflour
1 free range egg, beaten

Cut the kernels from the sweetcorn by standing the upright each in a bowl and cutting downwards with a sharp knife. Put the kernels and the cobs into a pot and cover with 1.5 litres of water and the salt. Bring to the boil and then simmer for 20 minutes. Remove and discard the cobs and blitz the corn to a smooth purée. Strain through a sieve and set aside.

If you are using tinned corn, empty the tins into a pot and add enough water to make it 1.5 litres. Add a good pinch of salt. Bring to the boil and then blitz to a smooth purée. Strain through a sieve and set aside.

In a saucepan, heat the sesame oil and add the spring onions, ginger and chilli and cook gently for a few minutes to soften. Add the sherry or Chinese rice wine and cook for a further minute. Add the crabmeat and the sweetcorn purée and bring to a simmer.

In a small bowl, mix the cornflour with a spoonful of the soup liquid to make a smooth paste. Return this to the pan and simmer together for 10 minutes for the soup to thicken slightly and the flavours to blend.

Remove the soup from the heat, taste and adjust the seasoning. When it has cooled slightly, pour the beaten egg into the soup in a steady stream, whisking all the time to create thin, silky strands throughout the liquid. Taste for seasoning before serving with a little spring onion sprinkled on top.

CRAB BRIK

Serves 4
as a main
or 8 as
starters

300g white crabmeat
50g brown crabmeat
1 red chilli, deseeded and finely chopped
3–4 sprigs of mint, leaves picked
small bunch of coriander, leaves picked and chopped
small bunch of parsley, leaves picked and chopped
1–2 tbsp lemon juice
½ tsp cumin
salt and ground pepper
1 litre sunflower oil
lemon wedges and harissa paste, to serve

You will need 12 sheets of 20cm-square filo pastry, a pastry brush and a cooking thermometer.

Mix the crabmeat with the spices, herbs and lemon juice. Season well. Divide the crab mixture into four. Wrap a portion of the crab mixture in the filo pastry and brush with a little water. Repeat until you have wrapped three filo sheets around it. Now do the same with the other three portions.

Line a plate with kitchen paper and set aside. Heat the oil in a deep saucepan to about 180°C/350°F. Using a slotted spoon, carefully place each parcel in the hot oil for 3–4 minutes or until golden. Remove with a slotted spoon and drain on the kitchen paper. Serve with the lemon wedges and harissa paste.

DRESSED CRAB

Picking a crab can be fun and very satisfying but it does require a bit of patience. Many more fishmongers now sell picked crabmeat more often that whole crabs. If you don't feel like picking the crab yourself, this is a perfect alternative.

Serves 4

1.5–2kg brown crab, cooked
squeeze of lemon juice
1 tsp olive oil
salt and pepper

Mayonnaise
2 egg yolks
2 tbsp white wine vinegar
2 tbsp Dijon mustard
300ml olive oil
squeeze of lemon juice

Herb salad
200g mixed salad leaves
mixed handful of basil, mint
    and parsley leaves
juice of ½ lemon
100ml extra virgin olive oil
salt and pepper

To pick the crabmeat, place it on its back on a board. Snap off the claws by pulling them back, away from the main shell. Separate the body from the main shell by pulling back the strip that comes up from the bottom of the crab and lies flat along its belly. Then prise the body away from the main shell by putting your thumbs under the edge of the shell and pushing upwards. You will hear a crack and the body will release. Pull the soft 'dead man's fingers' away from the body, and discard them.

Pour away any excess water from the main shell and scrape the brown meat into a bowl. Mash lightly with a fork. Using a crab pick or a suitable thin sharp utensil, pick the white meat from the cavities inside the body. The more meat you remove, the more you will see where it is hidden. Eventually you will have a body of empty cavities and a pile of white crabmeat.

The claws are the easier part! Crack the shell of the claws using a light hammer or a nutcracker and gently pull the meat away from the cartilage.

Finally, mix all the white meat together and gently run your fingers through to find any cracked pieces of shell. Dress the white and brown meat separately with lemon juice, olive oil and salt and pepper.

Make the mayonnaise by whisking the yolks in a bowl with the vinegar and mustard. Slowly pour in the olive oil in a thin stream, whisking all the time until you have a thick emulsion. Season with a little lemon juice, salt and pepper and set aside.

Mix the salad leaves and herbs in a bowl and dress with lemon, olive oil and salt and pepper. To serve, put a spoonful of both white and brown crabmeat on a plate with a good pile of salad and a dollop of mayonnaise. Accompany with bread and butter on the side.

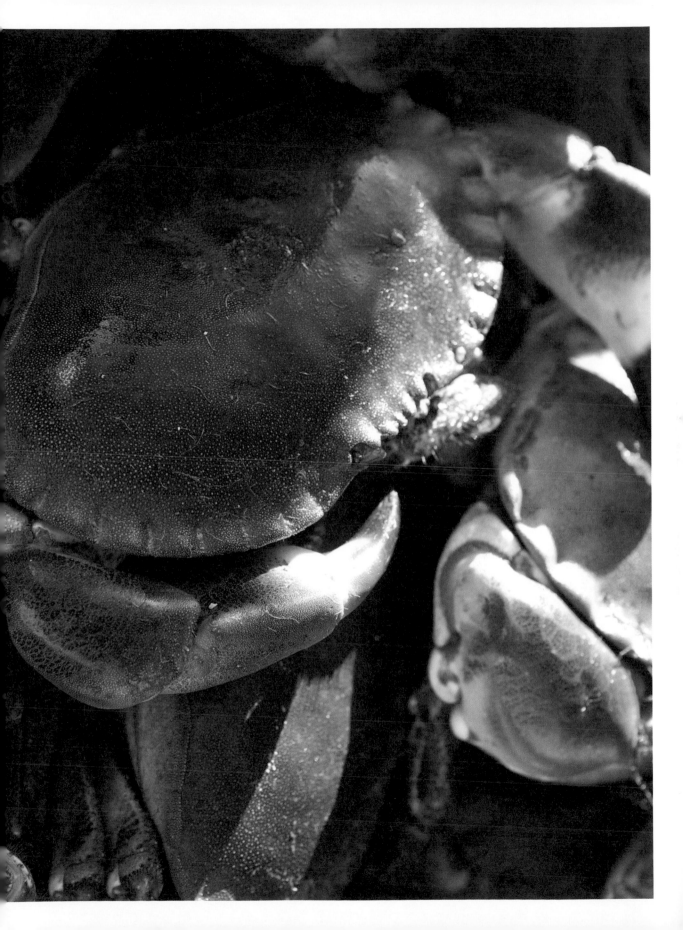

POTTED CRAB

Makes 4
ramekins

400g white crabmeat
50g brown crabmeat
nutmeg, grated
¼ tsp ground mace

½ tsp Tabasco sauce
juice of ½ lemon
salt and pepper
100g unsalted butter, melted

Preheat the oven to 150°C/300°F/Gas 2. Mix the white and brown crabmeat together and grate in some nutmeg. Add the mace, Tabasco sauce and lemon juice. Season well with salt and pepper and mix thoroughly. Divide the crabmeat between the four ramekins.

Pour enough melted butter into each ramekin just to cover the crabmeat mixture. Put the ramekins in a roasting tin and pour in boiling water to surround them and come halfway up the sides of the ramekins. Bake for 10 minutes. Remove and leave to cool before refrigerating to allow the butter to set completely. These will keep in the fridge for up to 3 days.

MADAGASGAN CRAB CURRY

Serves 4

3 brown, cooked large crabs,
  about 4.5–5kg in total
2 tbsp olive oil
6 spring onions, finely sliced
1 garlic clove, sliced
1 small knob of root ginger,
  peeled and grated
1 red chilli, deseeded and
  finely chopped
pinch of salt

400g butternut or crown prince
  squash, peeled and grated
½ tsp each ground cumin, turmeric,
  ground coriander, ground cinnamon
  and ground black pepper
400g tin chopped tomatoes
400ml tin coconut milk
small bunch of coriander, roughly
  chopped, tough stems discarded

First prepare the crabs. You could ask your fishmonger to do it for you and, if you do, ask him to break the claws from the body and crack them for you.

To separate the body from the main shell pull back the strip that comes up from the bottom of the crab and lies flat along its belly. Then prise the body away from the main shell by putting your thumbs under the edge of the shell and pushing upwards. You will hear a crack and the body will release. Pull the soft 'dead man's fingers' away from the body, and discard them. Pour away any excess water from the main shell. Scrape the brown meat into a bowl and mash it lightly with a fork. Chill the crabmeat in the fridge until needed.

In a large casserole (big enough to fit all the crab bodies), heat the olive oil. Add the spring onions, garlic, ginger and chilli and a pinch of salt and cook gently for a couple of minutes or until the onion and garlic become soft and slightly coloured. Add the squash and all the spices and continue to cook for a couple more minutes.

Add the tomato and cook for about 5 minutes until slightly reduced and thickened. Add the coconut milk and the brown crabmeat. Stir well and cook for another 5 minutes, allowing the sauce to come to the boil before turning it down to a simmer.

Taste the sauce, adjust the seasoning and then add the cracked crab bodies. Stir to coat with the sauce and cook slowly for 5 minutes or so to allow all the flavours of the sauce to be absorbed into the crab.

Serve in a large bowl sprinkled with coriander, with coconut rice on the side.

SPICY CRAB SALAD

Serves 2

Dressing
juice of 1 lime
1 tbsp soy sauce
1 tsp fish sauce
1 tbsp rice wine vinegar (Mirin)
2 tbsp vegetable oil
1 tsp sugar
½ red chilli, deseeded and chopped
salt and pepper

Salad
200g white crabmeat
½ cucumber, deseeded and chopped
1 avocado, sliced
1 spring onion, finely chopped
2–3 sprigs of mint, leaves picked and chopped, stems discarded
small bunch of coriander, chopped, tough stems discarded

Place all the dressing ingredients into a bowl and whisk together well. Adjust the seasoning as necessary.

Add all the salad ingredients to a large salad bowl and mix gently. Pour over the dressing. Toss together gently and serve.

POTATO

POTATO
with RECIPES *by* GREGG WALLACE

From creamy buttery mash to crisp golden chips or velvety smooth soups, the simple potato appears in many different guises. Not only do the different varieties come in beautiful shapes and different colours and sizes but each variety cooks in a particular way, lending itself perfectly to different types of dishes. Pink Fir Apple and Ratte are firm and waxy and perfect for salads, whereas the dramatically purple-skinned Arran Victory makes a milky white mash with an exceptional flavour.

The potato is the king of the vegetable world. For generations, its unique versatility has been celebrated and it has found its place at the heart of British cuisine. But potato sales are in decline and the tastiest and most unexpected varieties are under threat. Many people have begun to view the potato as an unhealthy alternative to rice or pasta when the truth is the reverse. Potatoes are not only delicious, they contain vital minerals and vitamins needed for a healthy, balanced diet.

The most flavoursome varieties have struggled to find shelf space in our over-regulated supermarkets, where varieties are chosen for their crop yield and convenience and not for their taste. Thankfully, heritage growers are reviving strains from the past. Today, varieties such as Salad Blue, Mr Little's Yetholm Gypsy and Ratte are being grown more widely.

Looking for specific, named varieties and choosing the right one for a recipe is worthy of the time well spent. This king of ingredients will really make a difference to a humble dish and offer a marvellous and welcome subtlety to a hearty supper.

GNOCCHI
and TOMATO SAUCE

I love making this, it reminds me of Play-Dough when I was a kid. Controversy rages over the inclusion of an egg. Some say yes, some no and some insist it should just be a yolk. I prefer to omit the egg. (Interestingly, the French do and the Italians don't.) The egg does help to bind the mixture together, but then it does make the gnocchi heavier. Once you've mastered perfect gnocchi you'll find they work brilliantly with hundreds of sauces. *Gregg Wallace*

Serves 4

Gnocchi
300g potatoes
50g plain flour

Tomato sauce
small glug of olive oil
1 small onion, finely diced
1 garlic clove, finely chopped
1 tbsp tomato purée
400g tin of chopped tomatoes
pinch of sugar
basil leaves, to garnish

You will need a potato ricer.

Boil the potatoes with their skins on until cooked. Drain and set aside to cool.

Once the potatoes are cool, peel and put through a potato ricer until you have reached 250g. Meanwhile, put a large pot of salted water on to boil.

Place the riced potatoes on a floured surface and knead in the flour. When a sort of dough forms divide it into quarters and roll out four shapes about the size of an average sausage. Cut into pieces 2.5cm long. Then press each piece with a fork to create a lined pattern.

To make the tomato sauce, heat the olive oil in a small saucepan and add the onion and garlic. Add the tomato purée and tinned tomatoes and simmer for a couple of minutes. Then turn the heat to the lowest setting and stir occasionally.

Place the gnocchi into boiling water and cook for just a few minutes or until they rise to the top. Drain and serve with tomato sauce, garnished with the basil.

POTATO DAUPHINOISE

This – like many good potato recipes – is easy to make, but its delivery is big. Garlic features heavily here, but you have to decide for yourself how much you want: your palate doesn't lie to you. Me, I like lots. If you want it to be pretty and professional looking, you can use a ring to cut the potatoes out of the dish. I prefer mine spooned out in a style I like to call farmhouse. However you serve this, layers of creamy, steaming potatoes flavoured with salt and garlic are a joy to behold. *Gregg Wallace*

Serves 4
- 2 garlic cloves, peeled
- 10g sea salt
- 500g Maris Piper potatoes, sliced
- 300ml double cream
- 300ml milk

Preheat the oven to 180°C/350°F/Gas 4. Cut one of the garlic cloves in half and rub it around the inside of a 1.2 litre ovenproof dish and set aside.

With the flat of the end of a knife make a paste out of all the garlic cloves with the sea salt. Layer the sliced potatoes with the mashed garlic in the ovenproof dish and set aside. Combine the milk and cream in a jug and pour it over the sliced potatoes and mashed garlic. Place in the oven and cook for 1 hour and 45 minutes or until tender, golden and bubbling.

SHEPHERD'S PIE

Well worth becoming a shepherd for, here is one of the world's truly great inventions – soft, moist pieces of lamb and firmer little bits of veg, all topped with creamy mashed potatoes. I used leftover roast lamb here, but minced lamb from the shops does a very decent job. (If you use the leftover gravy too, omit the flour in the recipe.) I've also added a good many flavourings, but I urge you to add what's right for you. I will also let you in to a guilty secret: I find it really hard to eat lamb without mint sauce. And just one plea – do not be tempted to put cheddar on the top. When was the last time you ate lamb and cheese? *Gregg Wallace*

Serves 4

2 medium onions, quartered
2 medium carrots, quartered
2 celery sticks, quartered
2 garlic cloves, peeled
4 tbsp rapeseed or olive oil
450g roast lamb
1 tbsp plain flour
150ml red wine
1 tsp thyme leaves
4 tsp Worcestershire sauce
1 tsp anchovy essence

1 tsp mushroom ketchup
1–2 tsp redcurrant jelly, (optional)
400g tin chopped tomatoes
300ml lamb stock or gravy
salt and pepper

Mash
750g masher potatoes, peeled and
    cut into medium-sized chunks
50ml milk
50g butter
salt and pepper

Preheat the oven to 200°C/400°F/Gas 6. Tip all the vegetables into a food processor and pulse. Heat the oil in a very large frying pan or casserole and add the vegetables. Cook over a medium heat for 15–20 minutes until softened but not browned.

Pulse the lamb in the food processor and add to the vegetables. Heat through for 2 minutes and stir in the flour and cook for a further 2 minutes. Pour in the wine, turn up the heat and leave to bubble away for 3–4 minutes. Add the thyme, Worcestershire sauce, anchovy essence, mushroom ketchup, redcurrant jelly if using, tomatoes and stock or gravy, and bring to a boil. Reduce the heat, season to taste with a little salt and freshly ground black pepper and let it simmer uncovered for 20 minutes.

Meanwhile, place the potatoes in a medium-sized pan and cover with cold water. Bring to a boil for 15 minutes or until cooked through. Drain well and return to the pan. Add the milk and butter, and mash together. Season to taste with salt and freshly ground black pepper.

Pour the lamb into an ovenproof dish, spoon over the potato and smooth with the back of a spoon. Cook in the oven for 20 minutes until golden brown. If you have prepared the shepherd's pie in advance and are reheating it, you will need to leave it in the oven for 40 minutes at 180°C/350°F/Gas 4.

POTATO *and* LEEK SOUP

Serves 4–6
40g butter
350g leeks, trimmed and sliced
1 white onion, sliced
salt and pepper
350g Yukon Gold potatoes, cut into 1cm chunks
1 litre chicken or vegetable stock
200ml single cream
small bunch of chives, chopped

In a saucepan, melt the butter and add the leeks and onion and a little salt. Cook gently for 4–5 minutes or until the leeks are soft and sweet but not brown. Add the potatoes and stir to coat with the butter. Season well and cook for a couple of minutes. Add the stock and bring to the boil. Turn down to a simmer and cook for about 6–7 minutes or until the potato is completely soft.

Place the mixture into a blender and purée until smooth, then strain through a sieve back into the pan. Adjust the seasoning and add most of the cream. Heat to a simmer and cook for a couple of minutes. Serve sprinkled with chopped chives and the rest of the cream drizzled on top.

SEABASS
ROASTED *over* POTATOES
and FENNEL *with* HERBS

Serves 4   2kg sea bass, scaled and cleaned (a fishmonger will do this)
            salt and pepper
            1 lemon, sliced
            few sprigs of thyme
            700g small, waxy potatoes, such as Ratte or Charlotte
            2 fennel bulbs, weighing about 600g, trimmed and sliced lengthways
            small bunch of marjoram, leaves picked, stems discarded
            60ml olive oil
            150ml white wine

Preheat the oven to 200°C/400°F/Gas 6. Season the fish inside and out. Put 2–3 slices of lemon and all of the thyme inside the cavity and set aside.

Put the potatoes in a pan of salted water and boil for 8 minutes or so until nearly cooked. Drain and cool slightly before slicing into discs about 1cm thick. Bring another pan of salted water to the boil. Add the fennel and boil for about 3 minutes, then drain.

In a large bowl, mix the sliced potatoes and fennel with the marjoram, salt and pepper and most of the olive oil. Spread this mixture over the base of a baking tray. Place the fish on top and pour over the wine and the remaining oil. Arrange the rest of the lemon slices on the fish.

Roast in the oven for about 30 minutes or until the flesh is firm to the touch and the eyes are white. (A good way to test a whole fish is to insert a skewer through the thick part of the back. If there is no resistance, the fish is cooked.) The potatoes and fennel should be golden brown and crisp around the edges.

CHIPS *in* DUCK FAT

Serves 4–6   500g King Edward potatoes, sliced into chips
                    400g jar duck fat (this can be reused)
                    sea salt

Rinse the cut potatoes in cold water and drain. Lay them out on a kitchen towel and dab dry. Line a platter with kitchen paper and set aside. Heat the duck fat in a large saucepan to 130°C/250°F.

Fry the potatoes in the fat, in small batches, for about 4 minutes or until cooked all the way through but not browned. Lift out the fat with a slotted spoon and drain on the kitchen paper.

Increase the heat of the oil to 180°C/350°F and cook the chips in batches again for another 2 minutes or so or until browned all over. Remove and drain on kitchen paper. Sprinkle well with salt and serve piping hot.

POMMES PURÉE

Serves 4–6   450g Arran Victory or Red Duke of York potatoes, washed, skin on
                    1 tsp salt
                    240ml full fat milk
                    170g unsalted butter
                    salt and pepper

You will need a potato ricer.

Put the potatoes in a large saucepan, cover with cold water and add the salt. Bring to the boil and cook for 25–30 minutes or until a fork inserted into one meets no resistance. Drain and leave to cool slightly, but not completely, before peeling off the skins.

Squeeze the potatoes through the potato ricer into a clean saucepan. Heat very gently, stirring constantly to evaporate any excess water. In a separate saucepan, heat the milk and melt the butter into it.

When the milk is hot, pour it into the potatoes in a steady stream, whisking vigorously all the while until all the liquid is incorporated and the potatoes are completely smooth. You can add more hot milk if necessary. Season well to taste with salt and pepper and serve.

PATATAS BRAVAS

Serves 4–6   2 tbsp olive oil, for frying
1 Spanish onion, finely sliced
2 garlic cloves, sliced
1 red chilli, de-seeded and sliced
2 tsp sweet paprika
1 tin of plum tomatoes
500g potatoes, cut into 2cm chunks
   (something floury like a Dunbar Rover is excellent)
4 tbsp olive oil, for roasting
Salt and pepper
1 tbsp chopped parsley, to serve

In a frying pan, heat the oil and cook the onion with a little salt for a few minutes or until soft and sweet. Add the garlic and chilli and continue to cook for a minute or so. Add the paprika and the tomatoes and cook together for about 5 minutes until you have a thick sauce. Remove from the heat and season with salt and pepper. Set aside until needed.

Preheat the oven to 220°C/425°F/gas 7. Put the potatoes in a roasting tin and pour over the oil. Season with salt and pepper and roast for 15 minutes or until crisp and brown on the outside and soft inside.

When you are ready to serve, pile the potatoes into a bowl, pour over the tomato sauce and sprinkle with chopped parsley.

Serve as a shared plate with cocktail sticks or forks to eat with.

POTATO SALAD
with HERRING

Serves 4–6   900g small waxy potatoes, such as Ratte or Pink Fir Apple
½ tsp salt
½ red onion, sliced finely
2 carrots, sliced finely into rounds
200g mâche lettuce
6–8 pickled herring fillets, sliced

Vinaigrette
½ garlic clove, crushed
1 tsp Dijon mustard
2 tsp red wine vinegar
90ml olive oil
salt and pepper

Boil the potatoes in salted water until they are soft. Meanwhile, make the vinaigrette by mixing the garlic, mustard and vinegar in a bowl and then whisking in the olive oil. Season well to taste.

When the potatoes are cooked, drain and leave until they are cool enough to handle. Slice them into pieces thick enough to hold together but not too thick. In a serving bowl, mix the potatoes gently with the onion, carrot and lettuce and dress with the vinaigrette. Add the herring slices and pile onto a plate to serve.

POTATOES
with SALSA VERDE

Serves 4–6
600g small, waxy potatoes, such as Pink Fir Apple
bunch each of parsley and basil, leaves picked from stem, finely chopped
2–3 sprigs each of mint and oregano, leaves picked, finely chopped
50ml extra virgin olive oil
1 garlic clove, crushed to a paste with salt
50g capers, chopped
50g anchovies, chopped
2 tsp Dijon mustard
1 tbsp red wine vinegar
salt and pepper

Cook the potatoes in plenty of boiling, salted water for 10 minutes or so until soft.

Put the chopped herbs into a bowl and add the extra virgin olive oil. Stir well to coat to prevent their discolouring.

Stir in the garlic paste, capers and anchovies. Add the mustard and finally the vinegar and mix well. Season to taste. Pour over the potatoes and mix well to coat them.

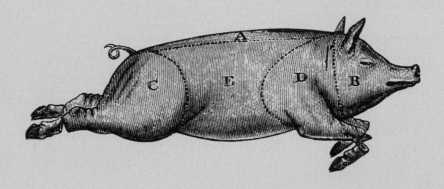

PORK

PORK
with RECIPES *by*
CLARISSA DICKSON WRIGHT

Think of crisp, salty crackling, succulent pork chops or meltingly tender pork belly. There are so many wonderful dishes and ways to cook with pork. Perhaps more than any other meat, the quality of the animal makes all the difference. It's very simple; well fed and reared animals have a much better taste and with pork, so much of that flavour and juiciness comes from creating good-quality fat on a well cared for porker.

It is a truth widely known that rare breed pigs provide a far superior meat to that of their commercially bred cousins. But these delicious beasts are under threat. Slow-grown breeds such as the Dorset Gold Tip, the Cumberland and the Lincolnshire Curly Coat gradually disappeared and part of our farming heritage was lost.

Now, though, measures are being put in place to save those varieties on the brink of extinction. The British Saddleback and Tamworth breeds have slowly been vanishing from our food chain, but the British Lop has been brought back from the edge, by breeders such as Jan McCourt of Northfield Farm in Rutland. However, with only a few hundred breeding females being reared we, as consumers, need to create the demand for these very special animals to be kept.

In 2010, Gloucestershire Old Spot was awarded the coveted TSG (Traditional Speciality Guaranteed) status by the European Union. This is a formal acknowledgement of quality and ensures that the breed is kept pure. Strict farming methods must be adhered to and this helps to produce tastier and juicier meat than can be achieved with conventional pigs.

Traditional breeds are now being featured on many restaurant menus around the country. A good butcher will stock them or be able to source them for you.

At the heart of this revival, alongside much of the other produce in this book, is the need to understand what we are eating. Only then can we really appreciate the quality and nature of our traditional breeds. Cost is always an important consideration but sometimes it's simply worth it for a superior product. Alternatively, purchase a little less meat but enjoy the delicious, more complex flavour. You will be truly rewarded with astounding pork that has been lovingly farmed.

STUFFED SHOULDER OF PORK

Shoulder is a reasonably priced cut of pork and, with the British Lop or heritage breeds in general, there will be enough fat to give you good crackling. You can, if you prefer, stuff a cut of the leg instead. You can vary the stuffing to suit your taste and store cupboard but make sure you include something like the lemon juice, rind and capers to lift the taste. If you want more stuffing you can make the surplus mixture into balls and cook them around the meat.
Clarissa Dickson Wright

Serves 6   2kg boned shoulder of pork

Stuffing
3 tbsp olive oil, plus extra for rubbing
1 onion, finely chopped
4 slices of white bread, crusts removed, cut into 1cm dice
75g walnuts, chopped
2 tsp small capers
juice and zest of 1 lemon
5 fresh sage leaves, chopped
salt and pepper
1 large free range egg, to bind

Preheat the oven to 230°C/450°F/Gas 8. Heat the olive oil in a large frying pan over a medium heat and gently fry the onion until soft and translucent. Add the breadcrumbs and fry for a further 2–3 minutes. Remove from the heat.

Stir in the walnuts, capers, lemon juice and zest and sage leaves, and season. Allow to cool for 10 minutes. Then, break the egg into the pan and mix thoroughly to coat all the ingredients.

Lay the pork skin-side down and spread the stuffing over the meat. Roll it up and tie securely with string. Make scores 2cm apart in the skin using a sharp knife, and rub with salt and oil.

Set the pork on a roasting tray and place in the oven. After 25 minutes turn the heat down to 170°C/325°F /Gas 3. Roast for a further 1 hour and 20 minutes then test with a skewer. When cooked the pork juices run clear. Remove from the oven and cover with tin foil. Allow to rest for 10 minutes before slicing and serving with mashed potatoes and gravy.

BELLY OF PORK
with ANCHOVY *and* CHESTNUTS

British Lop pork, used for this recipe, comes from an old breed of pig that has a good, even covering of fat, so that the belly is not excessively fat. With commercial pigs the belly is usually the only part with any fat at all. The use of anchovies with meat is a feature of the late eighteenth century and does not leave a fishy taste but adds depth to the dish. You will not need to add extra salt, as the anchovies will provide it. The chestnuts are a nice feature and provide a good texture. You can either buy pre-peeled sous vide nuts or keep your children occupied peeling chestnuts. In the latter case, cross the base of the nuts and put them into boiling water for a few minutes then run under a cold tap, drain and peel. Instead of deglazing the pan you can flambé a ladle of brandy and set fire to the contents, burning off any remaining fat. This also enhances the taste. *Clarissa Dickson Wright*

Serves 4–6   1 tin of anchovies
              3 tbsp olive oil, plus extra for rubbing
              1 onion, chopped into 1cm dice
              1 large garlic clove, chopped
              200g chestnuts, cooked, peeled and roughly chopped
              salt and pepper
              150ml dark beer (not stout)
              1.5kg belly of pork

Preheat the oven to 230°C/450°F/Gas 8. Gently heat a roasting pan and pour in the oil from the anchovy tin, and add the olive oil. Fry the onion and garlic for 2–3 minutes.

Chop the anchovies and add them, with the chestnuts, to the pan. Add a good grind of fresh black pepper and pour in the beer.

Score the rind of the pork with a sharp knife, slicing the scores 1cm apart, and rub with salt and oil.

Set the pork in a roasting pan so it covers the chestnut mix. Place in the oven and roast for 30 minutes. Then turn the temperature down to 170°C/325°F/Gas 3 and roast for a further 30 minutes. Serve the pork sliced with the chestnut mixture spooned over the top.

DAMSON PIES

The only raised fruit pie with a hot water crust that I have come across, made with gooseberries, is known as the Hungerford Pie. I invented Damson Pies for the programme to illustrate the use of lard in pastry making and to show the continued versatility of the pig. A few years ago there was a lard shortage as Poland had bought all of ours, and so there were no mince pies to be bought! If you still don't think you eat lard, do you enjoy smoothies? Most of them are emulsified with lard. Instead of membrillo (quince paste) you could use damson cheese (paste). But you will have to make it yourself for this recipe. I think these little pies work very well, especially with lashings of cream. *Clarissa Dickson Wright*

Serves 4–6
450g plain flour
1 tsp fine salt
200g pork lard
175ml water
250g damsons, stoned
150g caster sugar
2 slices of membrillo or damson cheese
clotted cream or crème fraiche, to serve

You will need a quarter-pound pie dolly for 4 pies or a half-pound pie dolly for 2 pies.

Sift the flour and salt together into a bowl. In a pan, heat the lard and water together until the lard has completed melted. Pour the water and lard mixture onto the flour and stir with a wooden spoon until it becomes a smooth and malleable pastry.

Once cool enough to handle, place the pastry on a flat surface and put the dolly in the middle. Mould the pastry up the dolly until you have an even thickness, saving enough pastry for the lid. Repeat the method for either 1 more or 3 more pies and gently place in the fridge to set.

Meanwhile, heat the damsons with the sugar over a low heat until the sugar has dissolved but the fruit still retains some shape. Remove from the heat.

Preheat oven to 220°C/425°F/Gas 7. Once the pastry is set in shape, place on a baking tray, remove the dolly and place a slice of membrillo in the bottom. Pour in the damsons and then lay another slice of membrillo on top.

For each pie, shape the lid to fit, with a small amount extra, and place on top. Press the lid and the base together then neatly fold the seam over to create a crust. Put a small slit in the lid to allow steam to escape, and place in the oven for 45 minutes. Serve with clotted cream or crème fraiche.

LINCOLNSHIRE STUFFED COLLAR

To prepare your own stuffed chine at home takes a considerable amount of work and a piece of chine is not very easy to get hold of outside the county of Lincolnshire. So here is a recipe for stuffed collar, the boneless equivalent. *Jim Sutcliffe, BBC Young Butcher of the Year*

Serves 2–4   1.5kg piece collar bacon, strings or netting removed
500g parsley, finely chopped

Using a sharp knife slice into the meat, lengthways, right down to the rind. Space these cuts about a thumb-width apart. Usually seven or eight cuts can be made into the average-sized collar. Once you have finished, your collar should look like an open book, with the slices being the pages.

Stuff the chopped parsley into the cuts, folding them back as you work across the joint. Once this is complete, tie up the joint by tying the strings back across the joint again at right angles to your stuffed cuts. Four or five strings should be sufficient.

Tie the stuffed collar tightly into a piece of muslin then place into a large pan of simmering water. Cover and simmer for approximately 40 minutes per kilogram plus 25 minutes. Once cooked allow it to cool in the cooking liquid overnight.

The next day, lift out of the liquid and unwrap it from the muslin. Wipe the jelly and lard off of the outside of the joint. To serve, slice the joint across the parsley stripes and enjoy it with a splash of malt vinegar or some English mustard. It is a delicious accompaniment to a salad and makes wonderful sandwiches.

SURPRISINGLY SIMPLE
PORK TERRINE

Serves 6–8   400g boned pork shoulder, chopped into 1cm chunks
              150g pig's liver, chopped
              400g pork belly, minced
              olive oil, for frying
              150g onion, diced
              salt and pepper
              small handful sage leaves, chopped
              ½ tsp each ground allspice and ground mace
              100g pistachio nuts, roughly chopped
              200g sliced streaky bacon, to line the tin

You will need a loaf tin approximately 20cm x 8cm or a terrine mould.

Preheat the oven to 180°C/350°F/Gas 4. Mix the pork shoulder, liver and minced belly together in a bowl and set aside. Heat a little olive oil in a frying pan and add the onion and a pinch of salt. Fry until it is soft and sweet but not too coloured. Add the sage leaves, allspice and mace and stir. Pour this into the meat mixture, along with the pistachios, and mix together. Season well with salt and pepper and set aside.

Line the loaf tin or terrine mould with the bacon, leaving some hanging over at either end. Carefully spoon in the meat mixture. Wrap the overhanging bacon over the top and cover with foil.

Place the tin or terrine mould in a roasting tin and fill with water so that it comes halfway up the sides. Bake for 1 hour and 30 minutes then remove from the oven. Leave to sit for 30 minutes before turning out.

PORK CHOPS
with SAGE, LEMON *and* BRAISED FENNEL

Serves 4

4 x 250g pork chops
8 slivers of lemon zest
juice of ½ lemon
small bunch of sage, leaves picked from stems and roughly chopped
salt and pepper
1 tbsp olive oil, plus extra
2 garlic cloves, sliced
2–3 sprigs of thyme
1kg fennel, trimmed and cut into quarters
50ml Pernod
1 tbsp parsley, chopped

Place the pork chops in a dish and rub them with the lemon zest, lemon juice, sage and plenty of black pepper. Set aside to marinate for 30 minutes.

Meanwhile, in a saucepan, heat the oil and fry the garlic until it is just beginning to brown. Add the thyme, fennel and Pernod and turn up the heat. Let it boil rapidly for a minute before turning the heat down again. Season with some salt and pepper and cook slowly with a lid on, stirring occasionally for about 25–30 minutes, or until the fennel is soft and stewed.

Heat the grill or a griddle pan and put a little oil and salt on the chops. Try to leave some of the sage and zest on the pork – when they cook with the meat they will give the dish extra flavour. Grill the pork chops for a couple of minutes on each side.

Meanwhile, remove the thyme from the fennel and discard. Stir the chopped parsley through the fennel. Serve the chops with the fennel and the cooking juices poured over.

RED BRAISED PORK

Serves 4

1kg pork belly, skin left on
1 tbsp groundnut or peanut oil
50g sugar
2 tbsp Chinese rice wine or white wine
100g spring onions, chopped
2 red chillies, deseeded and chopped
50g root ginger, peeled and sliced
6 star anise
5cm cinnamon stick
1 tbsp soy sauce
salt and pepper

Bring a large, heavy-bottomed pan of water to the boil and drop the pork belly into it. Skim off and discard any scum that rises to the surface and simmer for 30 minutes. Remove the meat from the liquid, drain and set aside. Clean the pan and return it to the heat.

Heat the oil in the pan and, when it is hot, add the sugar. Allow the sugar to melt and then start to turn dark brown and caramelise. Before it gets too dark, quickly pour in the wine. Add the spring onions, chillies and ginger, along with the spices. Return the pork to the pan and season well. Cover completely with water and bring to the boil. Turn down to a simmer and cook gently for up to 3 hours or until the pork is melting and tender.

Remove the pork from the pan and place it on a carving board. Strain the sauce through a sieve into a bowl. Return the strained sauce to the pan and turn up the heat. Boil rapidly to reduce the liquid to thick syrup. Taste for seasoning and add the soy sauce and some salt and pepper if desired. Cut the pork into 3cm cubes and return to the sauce. Serve with steamed pak choi.

BRAWN

Serves 8–10 as a starter

½ pig's head, cut into 2–3 pieces (ask your butcher to do this)
2 pig's trotters
1 head garlic, cut in ½ horizontally
300g carrots
300g celery
300g onion, halved
small bunch each of sage and thyme
2 bay leaves
8 black peppercorns
salt and pepper
juice of 1 lemon
small bunch of parsley, leaves picked from stems and chopped finely

You will need a terrine approximately 20 x 8cm.

Put the meat pieces and all the vegetables, herbs and peppercorns into a very large pan or stockpot, and cover with water. Bring to the boil then turn down to a simmer to cook for 3–4 hours. Keep an eye on the pan and top up with a little water if it is getting low. When it is ready, the meat will be falling away from the bone. Lift the meat from the liquid using a slotted spoon and set aside to cool.

Strain the liquid into a saucepan and boil to reduce to about 200ml. Season with salt and pepper and a little lemon juice. When the meat is cool enough to handle, pull it away from the bones and discard them, along with any bits of fatty skin. Chop the meat roughly and place in a bowl with the parsley leaves and mix well. Season with salt and pepper and the rest of the lemon juice, remembering it will be eaten cold, so you will need to season it more strongly.

Spoon the mixture into a terrine dish and pour over the stock so that it surrounds the chopped meat. Cover and refrigerate for 12 hours to set completely. Slice thickly and serve with cornichons and toast.

PORK PIE

Serves 4

Jelly
2 pig's trotters
1 large carrot, chopped into quarters
1 onion, quartered and stuck with 3 cloves
1 sprig each of thyme, sage and rosemary, plus a bay leaf,
    all tied together
6 black peppercorns
1.5 litres water
squeeze of lemon juice
salt and pepper

Hot-water crust
600g plain flour
½ tsp salt
250ml water
175g lard
1 free range egg, beaten

Filling
250g pork shoulder, boned
100g smoked streaky bacon, rind removed
250g pork belly, boned
1 tbsp sage, finely chopped
1 tsp thyme, chopped
1 bay leaf, ground to a powder
1 tsp ground allspice
½ tsp ground mace
1 tbsp anchovy essence
salt and pepper

Put all the jelly ingredients into a saucepan, except the lemon juice and salt and pepper and bring to the boil. Skim off any scum that rises to the surface and discard. Turn the heat down and leave to simmer gently for 2½–3 hours. Strain, return the liquid to the pan and bring to the boil. Continue to cook for another 20 minutes or so or until it has reduced by about half.

Season with salt, pepper and a squeeze of lemon juice. Set aside. Once cool, it will set to form a solid jelly. You will only need a small amount of this, but the rest you can use elsewhere or freeze.

To make the pastry, sift the flour into a bowl and mix with the salt. In a saucepan, heat the water and lard until all the lard has melted. Pour this in a steady stream into the flour, mixing all the time to form a soft ball of dough.

While it is still warm, reserve a small ball for the lid and press the rest of the pastry into a pie mould or a 14cm springform cake tin so that it covers the base and rises up the sides. Gently flatten the pastry you have kept back for the lid into a disc large enough to cover the top of the pie with a little remaining. Refrigerate all the pastry for at least 2 hours.

To make the pie filling, cut half of the shoulder into 1cm chunks. Mince or very finely chop the other half of the shoulder, the bacon and the pork belly. Mix all the meat together with the herbs, spices and anchovy essence and season well. Fry a teaspoon of the mixture and taste the flavour and seasonings. Bear in mind that you will be eating the pie cold so you need to make the flavour stronger than it tastes when hot.

Preheat the oven to 200°C/400°F/Gas 6. When the pastry has rested, fill the pie mould with the filling and place the lid on top. Join well around the sides with the pieces of overlapping pastry and cut a small hole in the centre of the lid. Brush the top with some of the beaten egg, keeping the rest for brushing the sides later.

Place on a baking tray and bake in the oven for 20 minutes. Then turn down the oven to 170°C/325°F/Gas 3 and bake for a further 45 minutes. Remove and very carefully release the pie from its mould or cake tin. Brush the sides with the remaining egg and return to the oven. After 10 minutes remove from the oven and set aside to cool.

To insert the jelly into the pie, you will need to gently heat it to liquefy it again. Pour the warm jelly through a funnel (you can even use rolled card for this) into the hole you made in the centre of the pie lid. Keep pouring until no more liquid can fit in. Place the pie in the refrigerator to cool completely and to allow the jelly to set before slicing. Serve with English mustard and pickles.

CHORIZO, MONKFISH *and* CHICKPEA STEW

Serves 4–6

200g smoked chorizo, sliced
2 garlic cloves, sliced
1 red onion, sliced
small bunch of thyme, leaves stripped and stems discarded
large sprig of rosemary, leaves stripped and chopped, stem discarded
400g tin peeled plum tomatoes
½ jar piquillo peppers or 4 red peppers, grilled, skinned and sliced
pinch of saffron, infused in 50ml boiling water
1 tsp smoked hot paprika
100ml dry sherry
250g cooked chickpeas
800g monkfish, cut into bite-sized chunks
salt and pepper

In a large casserole pan, brown the chorizo. Add the garlic, onion and thyme and rosemary leaves and cook together for 4–5 minutes to allow the onion and garlic to soften and brown slightly. Add the tomatoes, breaking them up with a wooden spoon. Cook to reduce to a thick sauce, about 5 minutes.

Add the peppers, saffron and paprika. Cook together for a minute or so before adding the sherry. Bring to the boil to allow the alcohol to evaporate and the sherry to reduce slightly. Stir in the chickpeas and a little water depending on how thick you would like the stew to be.

Bring the stew to the boil and finally add the monkfish pieces, adding a little more water if the stew is too thick. Turn down to a simmer and cook for a couple of minutes. The fish will continue to cook in the hot stew so it's better to take it off the heat when it is just cooked. Season to taste with salt and pepper and serve immediately in large bowls.

CAULIFLOWER

CAULIFLOWER
with RECIPES *by* THE HAIRY BIKERS

It is time to celebrate the cauliflower. Long hidden beneath the shadow of other more popular vegetables, it is now slowly making a welcome return. Often thanks to more exotic culinary influences, we can see what a versatile, delicate and delicious vegetable cauliflower can be: crunchy and raw in a fresh, lemony salad; soft and salty with a kick of chilli as pasta sauce; or a delicate, silky purée underneath a veal chop. Cauliflower not only looks pretty with its tight florets, it also offers wonderful options of texture and flavour.

The great British cauliflower has fallen out of favour so rapidly that sales dropped more than 35% over the past decade. According to a survey on eating habits it is one of the most disliked vegetables in the country. Cauliflower may have been grown in Britain since the late sixteenth century but it is facing stiff competition from popular green vegetables and is at risk of falling out of favour forever.

All too many of us have been left scarred by the memory of being forced to eat over-cooked cauliflower or school dinner cauliflower cheese. However, cooked with care, it is a versatile ingredient that is not only very tasty but contains large amounts of vitamins and dietary fibre. A well-executed cauliflower cheese is hard to beat; it is the perfect winter comfort food and a creamy teatime treat. But it can also be celebrated for its freshness in a delicious Indian curry or chargrilled in a Middle Eastern salad.

Cauliflower is one of the few vegetables that can be grown in the UK year-round. By choosing British cauliflower we can support our farmers and cut down on food miles. Modern innovations are making the process of growing and harvesting cauliflower easier too. Cooked well, cauliflower is not only delicious but it is surprisingly adaptable – even quite exotic – so there is no reason why it should not find favour again.

PERFECT CAULIFLOWER CHEESE
with BACON *and* MUSHROOMS

This is an adaptation of the traditional family recipe. My mother would always use a few mushrooms, and the addition of the Parmesan crumbs provide a great crunchy topping. You can also use Japanese panko breadcrumbs. Cauliflowers, apart from tasting great, are low in fat, high in fibre and full of vitamin C. We love them. They can be roasted, steamed, boiled, fried and even eaten raw. They are almost as versatile as a Hairy Biker. They also contain sulpherine, an anti-cancer compound released when the cauliflower is chewed or chopped. Lincolnshire is the most notable home of the cauliflower. Buy one today. Eat it, love it and smother it with cheese! This is a really satisfying main meal. Simply serve with salad and some crusty bread. *The Hairy Bikers*

Serves 4

1 medium-sized head of cauliflower, trimmed and broken into florets

Roux

250g smoked streaky bacon, cut into 1cm strips
250g chestnut mushrooms, finely sliced
25g butter
50g plain flour

250ml whole milk
pinch of English mustard powder
200g Gruyère cheese, grated
55ml double cream
salt and pepper
nutmeg, freshly grated

Topping

50g ciabatta breadcrumbs
50g Parmesan cheese, finely grated

Preheat the oven to 220°C/425°F/Gas 6. Place the cauliflower florets in a big saucepan of boiling water. Boil for about 10 minutes until just soft, drain and set aside in a large ovenproof dish. While this is happening, fry the bacon until coloured but not crisp. With a slotted spoon place the bacon pieces onto a plate and set aside, keeping the fat from the bacon in the frying pan. Sauté the mushrooms in the bacon fat until just taking on a bit of colour. Set aside.

Melt the butter in a saucepan and beat in the flour. Add the milk, stirring all the time, until you have a thick white sauce. Stir in the mustard powder and add the cheese and double cream, stirring all the time. Check the seasoning. Fold in the mushrooms and the bacon.

Pour the cheesy mushroom and bacon sauce on to the cauliflower florets and then grate over a little nutmeg. Mix the ciabatta crumbs with the Parmesan cheese, and sprinkle over the cauliflower to cover. Place in the oven for about 15 minutes until the sauce is bubbling and the crumbs are golden.

SEARED SCALLOPS *with* PANCETTA, CAULIFLOWER PURÉE *and* ORANGE-DRESSED ROCKET SALAD

A hearty everyday food, cauliflower has long been a favourite of fine diners too. The French have known this for years and so use cauliflower in many dishes including the fabulous Cremé Du Barry soup. This dish is a celebration of Lincolnshire, inspired by our filming on the *Food Tour of Britain*. Great scallops from the North Sea go fantastically well with the Lincolnshire Poacher Cauliflower Cheese Purée but please feel free to use your cheese of choice. Gruyère works well in this Coquilles St Cauliflower. *The Hairy Bikers*

Serves 4

Cauliflower purée
1 head Lincolnshire cauliflower, broken into florets
55ml double cream
150g Lincolnshire Poacher cheese, grated
sea salt and white pepper

Dressing and salad
55ml extra virgin olive oil
25ml white wine vinegar
55ml orange juice
zest of ½ an orange
1 tsp wholegrain mustard
bag of rocket leaves

Scallops
200g pancetta, thinly sliced
20 scallops, trimmed, corals removed
juice of 1 lime
sea salt flakes and black pepper

Place the cauliflower florets in a big saucepan of boiling water. Boil for about 10 minutes until just soft. Drain and set aside on a plate lined with kitchen paper to remove any water. (This recipe is better if the cauliflower is dry.) Place the florets in a food processor. Add the cream and cheese and purée until fine. Season to taste. Place in a piping bag and set aside for plating up. Now for the salad, combine the salad dressing ingredients in a large bowl and whisk to emulsify. Toss in the rocket leaves and set aside.

Fry off the thin pancetta slices until crispy and all the fat has rendered out. Remove from pan and, while still warm, cut in half and place to one side. Leave the pancetta fat in the pan to cook the scallops.

In the hot frying pan, sear the scallops each side for about a minute, depending on the size. (It is very easy to overcook scallops.) They should have a lovely caramelised colour on each side and be slightly firmer but not tough. Draw the pan off of the heat and squeeze over the juice of the lime. Season to taste.

Place a handful of leaves in the middle of each plate. Pipe five blobs of cauliflower purée around the salad. Set a piece of pancetta on the purée, then a perfectly cooked scallop on top of that. Serve immediately.

SAAG ALOO
with ROASTED GOBI

Cauliflower is an international vegetable, loved from Bangalore to Belgravia. The British introduced Cauliflower to India in the nineteenth century. (And did you know it was a Cornish variety?) Cauliflower is economical and quite a dense creature so it can make a satisfying main meal. There is very little water added to this dish – all the liquid comes from the veg. Something wonderful happens to cauliflower when it is roasted and then combined with a traditional Aloo Gobi (potato and cauliflower curry). It is a taste of magic. We wrote this recipe when filming in Chennai in India. A favourite vegetable dish of ours, this is great served with rice or used for stuffing Indian bread. We think it is the best we have tasted and worth a try. *The Hairy Bikers*

Serves 4

Roasted cauliflower
½ head white cauliflower,
   broken into florets
½ head Romanesco cauliflower,
   broken into florets
splash of olive oil
salt and pepper

Vegetable curry
55ml ghee or vegetable oil
1 onion, chopped finely
1 thumb-sized piece of root ginger, grated
1 tsp black mustard seeds

5 curry leaves, dried or fresh
½ tsp turmeric
½ tsp ground fenugreek
2 green chillies, left whole
½ tsp chilli powder
3 medium potatoes, peeled and
   diced into 2cm cubes
250g tomatoes, chopped
450g baby spinach leaves
½ tsp salt
½ tsp sugar
55ml water
squeeze of lemon juice

Preheat the oven to 180°C/350°F/ Gas 4. Coat the florets with oil and season. Place on a baking tray and roast for 20 minutes.

In a saucepan warm the ghee or oil and fry off the onion until transparent. Add the ginger, mustard seeds, curry leaves, turmeric, fenugreek, chillies and chilli powder.

Cook for 2 minutes, stirring continuously, until the seeds start popping. Add the potatoes, and stir through until coated by the spices. Add the tomatoes, spinach leaves, salt, sugar and water. Bring to a simmer for 20 minutes.

Stir the roasted cauliflower into the curry. Check the seasoning and finish with a squeeze of lemon juice. Serve with basmati rice.

OTTOLENGHI'S CHARGRILLED CAULIFLOWER
with TOMATO, DILL *and* CAPERS

Serves 2–4

2 tbsp capers, drained and roughly chopped

1 tbsp French wholegrain mustard

2 garlic cloves, crushed

2 tbsp cider vinegar

salt and pepper

120ml olive oil

1 small cauliflower, divided into florets

1 tbsp dill, chopped

50g baby spinach leaves

20 cherry tomatoes, halved

First make the dressing, either by hand or in a food processor. Mix together the capers, mustard, garlic, vinegar and some salt and pepper. Whisk vigorously, or run the machine, while adding half the oil in a slow trickle. You should get a thick, creamy dressing. Taste and adjust the seasoning.

Add the cauliflower florets to a large pan of boiling salted water and simmer for 3 minutes only. Drain through a colander and run under a cold tap to stop them cooking immediately. Leave in the colander to dry well. Once dry, place in a mixing bowl with the remaining olive oil and some salt and pepper. Toss well.

Place a ridged griddle pan over the highest possible heat and leave it for 5 minutes or until very hot. Grill the cauliflower in a few batches – make sure the florets are not cramped. Turn them around as they grill then, once nicely charred, transfer to a bowl. While the cauliflower is still hot, add the dressing, dill, spinach and tomatoes. Stir together well, then taste and adjust the seasoning. Serve warm or at room temperature, adjusting the seasoning again at the last minute.

CAULIFLOWER *and* CEP SOUP

Serves 4

2 tbsp olive oil

2 garlic cloves, sliced

200g floury potatoes, peeled and cubed

700ml water

salt and pepper

500g cauliflower, broken into florets and roughly chopped

300g cep mushrooms, stalks chopped, caps sliced, to garnish

40ml cream, to serve

Heat the oil in a large saucepan. Add the garlic and cook until it just starts to colour. Add the cubed potatoes and briefly fry. Pour over the water and season well. Bring to the boil for about 4 minutes or until the potatoes are almost cooked through.

Add the cauliflower and the cep stalks. Cook until everything is soft then, using a whisk or a potato masher, break up the vegetables so you have a semi-smooth soup. Season well and serve in separate bowls with a little cream and the sliced cep caps over the top.

CAULIFLOWER Á LA GRECQUE

Serves 4–6

1 green romanesco or white cauliflower,
  about 500g, broken into florets
pinch of salt
½ tbsp olive oil
½ white onion, finely sliced
1 tsp fennel seeds
2 tsp coriander seeds
¼ tsp peppercorns
200 ml white wine
200 ml water
juice of ½ lemon

Cook the cauliflower florets in plenty of boiling, salted water for about 3 minutes or until just tender on the outside. Drain and set aside. Heat the olive oil in a large saucepan on a low heat and add the onion and a pinch of salt. Fry until it is soft and sweet but not browned, about 5 minutes.

In a dry frying pan, lightly roast the fennel and coriander seeds so their fragrance rises and they start to crackle. This usually takes less than a minute, so be careful not to burn them. Add the seeds, along with the peppercorns, to the cooked onion. Stir well and cook together for a minute or so to infuse the flavours.

Add the cooked cauliflower and pour over the wine. Turn up the heat to boil the alcohol away. Then add the water, lemon juice and a little more salt. Turn the heat down and gently stir in the cauliflower to coat. Cook for a few minutes. Set aside in the liquid to cool and then serve as a side dish.

CAULIFLOWER
with CHILLI *and* ANCHOVY PASTA

Serves 4   1 medium-sized cauliflower, about 600g, broken into florets
             olive oil, for frying
             2 garlic cloves, sliced
             1 red chilli, finely chopped
             8 salted anchovy fillets
             salt and pepper
             250g dried penne
             2 tbsp extra virgin olive oil
             chopped parsley, to serve

Cook the cauliflower in plenty of boiling, salted water for 4–5 minutes or until it is soft. Drain away all the water except for a tablespoon or two.

Heat some olive oil in a pan and gently fry the garlic and chilli until the garlic is just starting to colour, then add the anchovies. Cook for a minute or so to allow the anchovies to melt into the oil. Add the cooked cauliflower and the reserved water, breaking the florets up gently with a wooden spoon.

Cook together for a few minutes until you have a soft, wet sauce. Season with pepper and just a little salt bearing in mind the saltiness of the anchovies. Cook the pasta in boiling, salted water for 10–12 minutes or until al dente. Drain and mix with the sauce. Pour over the extra virgin olive oil, sprinkle with the chopped parsley and serve.

FATTOUSH

Serves 6

2 pitta breads
40g butter, melted
1 cucumber, peeled, deseeded and diced
2 tomatoes, halved and seeds removed
bunch of radishes, quartered
1 small cauliflower, cut into small florets
½ red onion, thinly sliced
bunch of purslane or mâche lamb's lettuce, chopped
cos lettuce, core removed and leaves sliced
small bunch of parsley, roughly chopped
few sprigs of mint, roughly chopped
garlic clove, crushed to a paste with salt
juice of 1 lemon
1 tbsp sumac
125ml extra virgin olive oil
salt and pepper

Preheat the grill. Lay a pitta bread flat on a board, place one hand flat on top of it and cut it so that it opens into two thinner slices of pitta, of the same shape. Repeat with the other pitta. Brush the melted butter over both sides. Grill, turning once, until they are crisp and brown. Set aside.

Put all the chopped vegetables into a serving bowl. Add the purslane or mâche and sliced cos lettuce and mix well. Stir in the parsley and mint and set aside.

In a separate bowl, mix the garlic paste with the lemon juice. Add the sumac and stir well before mixing in the olive oil. Season well with salt and pepper to taste and set aside.

To serve, snap the crisp pitta into small pieces and stir into the vegetables. Pour the dressing over the top, add a little more salt and pepper and mix well. This is best eaten when the vegetables are still crunchy so don't let it sit around for too long.

CAULIFLOWER
with SWEET ONION, RAISINS *and* SAFFRON

Serves 4–6   salt and pepper
2 medium-sized cauliflowers, cut into small florets
3 tbsp olive oil
1 large red onion, thinly sliced
pinch of saffron
25g raisins
3 tbsp pine nuts

Bring a large saucepan of generously salted water to the boil and add the cauliflower florets. Boil for 2–3 minutes or until just tender, but still holding their shape. Drain and set aside to cool slightly.

Heat 1 tbsp of the olive oil in a large frying pan and add the onion. Add a good pinch of salt and cook gently until it becomes soft and sweet, about 10 minutes. Meanwhile, put the raisins in a little bowl and pour over enough boiling water to cover. This will plump them up and make them soft.

Put the saffron in an eggcup or small container and pour over 2 tablespoons of boiling water. Leave to infuse. Put the pine nuts in a dry frying pan over a medium heat to toast, tossing them so they brown evenly. Keep an eye on them as they burn easily. Once browned, set them aside.

Heat a griddle pan until it is very hot. Toss the cooked cauliflower in the remaining olive oil and griddle in batches so that the outside becomes slightly crisp and browned with griddle marks. When all the cauliflower is done, put it into a large serving bowl. Add the cooked onions, the saffron with its infusing water and the drained raisins. Season well and mix gently. Leave for 10 minutes or so for the flavours to blend. Add the toasted pine nuts and serve.

PICCALILLI

Makes 6 x
340g jars

300g each carrots, fennel, celery and runner beans, trimmed,
   peeled and cut into small, equally sized dice
300g small pickling onions, peeled
500g cauliflower, broken into small florets
100g salt
50g plain flour
20g each mustard seeds, ground ginger and turmeric
2 tsp coriander seeds, crushed
1 litre cider vinegar
200ml white wine vinegar
2 bay leaves
400g brown sugar

You will need six 340g jam jars.

Put the diced vegetables into a large bowl with the onions and cauliflower florets and pour over the salt. Mix well and then place in a colander set over a bowl. Cover and leave for 24 hours.

The next day, rinse the vegetables in cold water to remove the salt. Drain and set aside. Put the flour in a small bowl with the seeds and spices and mix well. Pour over a tablespoon of the cider vinegar, stir to make a thick paste and set aside.

In a large saucepan, pour in the rest of the cider vinegar, the white wine vinegar, bay leaves and brown sugar. Bring to the boil to dissolve the sugar. Put a few tablespoons of the hot vinegar mixture into the spice paste and stir to dilute. Pour this back into the vinegar mixture in the saucepan. Simmer the spiced vinegar for a couple of minutes.

Remove the bay leaves and stir in the vegetables. Take it off the heat, spoon into sterilised jars and seal immediately. (To sterilise the jars, wash and dry them thoroughly then heat them in an oven set at 150°C/300°F/Gas 2 for 10 minutes.) Store for at least six weeks before opening. This will keep for up to a year.

MUTTON

MUTTON
with RECIPES *by* MATT TEBBUTT

Fragrant, intense, served pink or slow cooked and meltingly tender – this is what mutton is really like. Mutton is one of the most misunderstood yet delicious of British meats. However, like all meat, it needs to be cooked and prepared with respect in order to bring out its finest texture and flavour.

As wine growers will tell you, maturity is a valuable thing when it comes to flavour. Mutton is meat from a sheep that is more than two years old but many believe the best meat comes from an animal at least five years old. Cooked well, it can be tender, rich and full of flavour. It can be hung and matured like beef but prepared badly the meat will take on a tough, chewy texture. It is the poor preparation of this deliciously aromatic meat that has created its so ill-deserved, bad reputation.

The roots of British distrust for mutton can be traced back to the end of World War II. Poor-quality mutton was one of the few types of meat readily available during rationing. As soon as other meats were in good supply, it was willingly forgotten. However, in 2004 the Mutton Renaissance campaign, spearheaded by Prince Charles, was founded to help revive this British heritage food. With new guidelines, campaigners have set an improved standard for quality, specifying that British mutton should be raised on a forage-based diet, including grass, heather and roots. Encouraged by this guarantee and passion, mutton has deservedly enjoyed a welcome return to our kitchens and dining tables.

From slow-cooked stews to broths, curries and braised dishes there are wonderful recipes to enjoy mutton's rich and complex flavour. Aged beef is highly prized and there is no reason why mutton, when farmed, aged and cooked properly, should not be equally valued. Sheep are part of Britain's farming heritage and our very landscape. The time has come to embrace all that mutton has to offer us.

BREAST OF MUTTON *with* LEEKS, EGG *and* MUSTARD VINAIGRETTE

This recipe is traditionally done with a lamb breast, but mutton works just as well. In fact, with its more developed flavour, I think using mutton actually improves this heritage dish. *Matt Tebbutt*

Serves 6

Mutton
1 breast of mutton
2 white onions, roughly chopped
1 head of celery, roughly chopped
2 leeks, roughly chopped
2 tsp salt
2 bay leaves
1 sprig of rosemary
1.2 litres lamb stock

Panee
200g plain flour

4 free range eggs, beaten
200g breadcrumbs

Vinaigrette
2 free range eggs
3 tbsp white wine vinegar
6 tbsp mild olive oil
3 heaped teaspoon Dijon mustard
3 garlic cloves, crushed

8 small leeks, blanched for 3 minutes
   until tender, to serve
6 salted anchovies, sliced, to serve

You will need a deep fat fryer, preferably with vegetable oil in or as recommended by the fryer's instructions.

Preheat the oven to 150°C/300°F/Gas 2. Lay the mutton breast in a large roasting tin, scatter over the vegetables, salt, bay leaves and rosemary. Pour over the stock. If it does not cover the meat, top it up with water. Place in the oven and simmer for 3 hours. Remove the meat from the stock and discard the bones. Press the meat between two baking trays under a heavy weight. Leave overnight in the fridge.

The following day, make the vinaigrette. Boil the eggs for 5 minutes and cool under cold running water. Peel and carefully take out the soft-boiled yolk. Place yolks in a mixing bowl, add the vinegar, oil, mustard and garlic, and lightly whisk together. Roughly chop the white of the eggs and gently fold into the mixture. Set to one side.

Trim the mutton into the toast soldier sizes. Preheat the deep fat fryer to 170°C/325°F. Prepare three bowls: one containing the flour, one with the beaten eggs and one with the breadcrumbs. Dip each 'soldier' into the flour, then the egg, then the crumbs and set on a plate. Repeat until all are coated.

Fry a few at a time for 2–3 minutes until golden brown, and place on a plate lined with kitchen paper. Keep warm in a low oven until all the mutton has been fried. Dress each plate with two small, halved blanched leeks, scattered with a sliced anchovy fillet. Place two mutton soldiers on each plate, drizzle with the vinaigrette and serve.

BOILED LEG OF MUTTON
with CAPER SAUCE

The Great British Classic – dishes like this – were once the staple of many households, but are now largely forgotten. Everything you need in a dish is here: rich, developed meaty flavours, salty capers and a silky cream sauce. This dish is part of our heritage and deserves to be celebrated. *Matt Tebbutt*

Serves 6–8

Mutton
1 leg of mutton
salt and pepper
200g butter
3 large onions, sliced
3 bay leaves
1 sprig of rosemary
10 black peppercorns
750ml white wine
600ml lamb stock

Caper sauce
600ml chicken stock
300ml double cream
1 small jar of capers
2 tbsp parsley, chopped
a buttered Cartouche, to stop skin layer
   from forming (optional)

You will need a piece of muslin and some kitchen string.

Preheat the oven to 150°C/300°F/Gas 2. Season the leg all over. Then generously rub the inside of the casserole dish with the butter. Place the leg into the casserole dish and set the sliced onions on top.

Wrap the bay leaves, rosemary and peppercorns in the muslin and tie with a piece of string into a little parcel. Place in the casserole dish. Pour in the white wine and lamb stock. Cover with a buttered Cartouche and place the lid on top. Put the casserole dish in the oven for 3 hours.

Towards the end of the cooking time, before serving, reduce the chicken stock by half. Add the cream and the capers. Simmer for two minutes. Season to taste, draw off of the heat and set aside.

Remove the mutton from the oven. Spoon the cooked onions onto a plate with a slotted spoon. Lay carved mutton slices on top. Spoon over the caper sauce and serve.

MUTTON SHOULDER TAGINE

This recipe has big powerful flavours that lend themselves to the fantastic mutton. The end result, after the long slow cooking, is a meltingly tender and hugely gratifying dish. *Matt Tebbutt*

Serves 6–8

1 mutton shoulder, on the bone
olive oil, for rubbing
salt and pepper
1 tbsp coriander seeds
½ tbsp cumin seeds
2 pinches of saffron
3 star anise
1 cinnamon stick
4 red onions, peeled and quartered
1 head of garlic, cloves separated, peeled and left whole
2 preserved lemons, quartered, inside flesh to be discarded
2 red chillies
2 x 400g tins chopped tomatoes
600ml lamb stock
1 bunch of coriander, roughly chopped, to garnish
1 bunch of mint, roughly chopped, to garnish

You will need a tagine with a heavy lid or a casserole pot.

Preheat the oven to 150°C/300°F/Gas 2. Rub the shoulder of mutton with olive oil, salt and pepper. Seal in a hot roasting pan and transfer to a tagine or casserole pot. Add the spices, onions, garlic, preserved lemons (removing the soft flesh inside), chillies and tinned tomatoes. Pour over the stock. Cover and cook in the oven for 3 hours.

When it has finished cooking, remove from the oven. Season with the remaining liquid with salt and pepper to taste and stir in the coriander and mint. Serve with cous cous.

LANCASHIRE HOT POT

Serves 4–6

Lamb stock
lamb bones from the rack
small bunch of thyme
1 bay leaf
6 black peppercorns
1 celery stick, halved
1 carrot, chopped
1 onion, halved
1.5 litres water
salt and black pepper

Hot pot
1kg rack of mutton, on the bone
   or 700g off the bone
1 tbsp olive oil
300g red onion, sliced
300g carrots, sliced
small bunch of thyme, leaves stripped
   and stems discarded
700ml mutton stock (either made
   with the bones or use a lamb stock cube)
800g potatoes, peeled and very thinly sliced
20g butter

To make your own stock, cut the mutton off the bone and put the bones into a large pot. Add the herbs and vegetables and cover with the water. Bring to the boil, skim off any scum that rises to the surface and discard. Turn down to a simmer and cook for at least 30 minutes. Strain into a bowl and return the liquid to the pot. Boil to reduce the stock to about 700–800ml. Taste, season with salt and pepper and set aside.

If you have not done so already to make the stock, cut the mutton off the bone and season all over. Heat the oil in an ovenproof casserole with a lid. Add the meat and brown well on all sides. Remove with a slotted spoon to a plate. Now add the onion, carrots, thyme and a pinch of salt and fry for several minutes or until soft and sweet. Return the mutton to the pan and cook together with the vegetables for a couple of minutes. Add the stock and season well.

Preheat the oven to 180°C/350°F/Gas 4. Place the thinly sliced potatoes on top of the meat in overlapping circles and season with salt and pepper. (If you manage two layers, season each layer.) Dot the butter in pieces over the top of the potatoes. Put on the lid and cook for about 1½–2 hours. Then remove the lid and continue cooking for another 30 minutes to brown the potatoes on top and serve.

LEG *of* MUTTON BAKED *in* HAY

Serves 6–8   3 or 4 handfuls of hay (from a farm or a pet shop)
150g softened butter
2 garlic cloves, crushed to a paste with salt
2 sprigs each of rosemary, thyme and marjoram, leaves stripped and
    roughly chopped, stems discarded
2kg leg of mutton
4 tbsp of redcurrant jelly
salt and pepper

Preheat the oven to 220°C/425°F/Gas 7. Choose a deep roasting tin, preferably with a lid. If you don't have a lid, you can use foil (see below). Line generously with about half of the loose hay to a thickness of about 5–6 cm and set aside.

In a bowl, mix the butter, garlic paste and herbs and set aside. Take the leg of mutton and smear the redcurrant jelly over it and then the herby butter mixture. Season well all over then place the leg on its bed of hay.

Cover with the rest of the hay and put on the lid. If you don't have a lid use two layers of foil wrapped well over the edge of the dish and pinched tightly in place. Make sure there are no loose bits of hay poking out.

Bake for 2½–3 hours. Remove from the oven and leave the meat to rest for at least 20 minutes. Take off the lid, remove the leg and scrape off the hay before carving.

MERGUEZ MUTTON SAUSAGES

Makes	500g mutton leg meat, minced
10–15	100g mutton fat
sausages	1 garlic clove, crushed to a paste with salt
	1 tbsp harissa paste
	1 tsp each ground cumin, ground cinnamon, ground ginger, and turmeric
	salt and pepper
	sheep sausage skins, for stuffing

You will need a Kitchen Aid with a sausage-stuffing attachment or a piping bag with a funnel.

Mix all the ingredients together (except the skins) and season well. Fry a spoonful of the sausage mix. Taste it and adjust the seasoning as necessary.

Soak the sausage skins in warm water for at least 20 minutes, drain and pat dry. If your Kitchen Aid doesn't have an attachment for stuffing sausages, you can stuff the skins by hand, using a piping bag with a funnel, or just make them into meatballs.

To stuff a skin, take one end and slide it over the end of the stuffing funnel. Knot the other end so the stuffing doesn't escape. Squeeze in enough mixture to make a sausage 15cm long. Twist the skin to seal and make a knot. Cut off the sausage and start the process again to make the next one. Try to stuff the skins as tightly as possible. You can always adjust this by squeezing the stuffing to one end and moving the knot.

To cook the sausages, fry in a little oil or grill. They are delicious served with cous cous or as part of a Moroccan stew.

MUTTON *and* TURNIP PIE

Serves 6–8

1kg mutton leg, boned and cut
  into 3–4cm pieces
salt and pepper
2 tbsp plain flour
3 tbsp olive oil
400g onions, sliced
300g celery, or 3–4 stalks, chopped
2–3 sprigs of rosemary, leaves stripped
  and roughly chopped, stems discarded

600g turnips, peeled and quartered
250ml white wine
300ml lamb or chicken stock
  (or water if you don't have any)

Pastry
600g puff pastry
flour, for dusting
1 free range egg, beaten

Preheat the oven to 180°C/350°F/Gas 4. Put the mutton pieces into a bowl and season with salt and pepper. Add the flour and toss to coat. Heat 2 tablespoons of oil in a large casserole and when it is smoking hot, add the floured mutton pieces and brown them briefly for a couple of minutes. You may need to do this in two batches. When all the pieces are browned, remove to a plate and set aside.

Turn down the heat under the casserole and add the remaining tablespoon of oil. Add the onion and celery with a pinch of salt and let them sweat for a couple of minutes until soft. Add the rosemary leaves and the turnip and cook for another couple of minutes.

Put the mutton back into the casserole and turn up the heat. Add the wine and boil for a minute or so before adding the stock. Check the seasoning and adjust if necessary. Cover the pot with a piece of baking parchment and the lid before putting it into the oven.

Cook for at least an hour before checking to see if the mutton is tender. If not, keep cooking. Different animals require different lengths of time so don't worry if you need to return it to the oven for another 30 minutes or so. When it is ready, the meat will be tender and there will be a good amount of juice around it. Remove from the oven and leave to cool.

When you are ready to cook the pie, preheat the oven to 180°C/350°F/Gas 4. Put the cooked mutton and all the vegetables and juice into a pie dish with a pie funnel in the middle. On a floured surface, roll out the puff pastry to about ½cm thick and lay it over the pie dish, making two little cuts where the funnel is, to allow the top to poke out.

With your thumb and forefinger, pinch around the edge of the dish to seal the pastry and make some decorative pinched grooves. Brush the pastry with the beaten egg and bake for about 30 minutes or until the top is golden and crisp.

RACK OF MUTTON STEWED *with* BORLOTTI BEANS *and* GARLIC

Serves 4

2 x 6-cutlet racks of mutton
salt and pepper
2 tbsp olive oil
200g each celery, carrots and shallots, sliced
100g garlic cloves, peeled
large sprig of rosemary
3–4 sprigs of thyme
2 bay leaves
800g cooked borlotti beans, rinsed
250ml red wine
300ml lamb or chicken stock

Preheat the oven to 180°C/350°F/Gas 4. Season the racks of mutton. In a large ovenproof saucepan, heat the oil and brown the racks on all sides, especially the skin side. Remove to a plate.

In the same pan, fry the celery, carrots and shallots with a pinch of salt for 3–4 minutes or until soft and sweet. Add the garlic cloves and cook for another minute or so. Add the herbs and the borlotti beans and mix well. Pour over the wine and bring to the boil. Boil rapidly for about a minute before adding the stock.

Lay the browned racks on top of the beans and cover loosely with foil. Place in the middle of the oven and cook for 1½ hours. Take off the foil and continue to cook for a further 20 minutes.

Lift out the mutton racks from the beans and set on a carving board. Remove the herb stems from the bean mixture and discard. Place a ladleful of beans and sauce onto four plates. Slice the racks into chops and place them on top of the beans to serve.

HARIRA

Serves 2

2 tbsp olive oil

300g mutton shoulder, cut into 1cm cubes

2 onions, sliced

200g celery, leaves and stalks, chopped

salt and pepper

1 tsp each ground cumin, ground cinnamon, ground ginger and turmeric

pinch of saffron

small bunch of parsley, leaves picked from stem and roughly chopped

400g tin pf plum tomatoes

1.5 litres water

50g dried red lentils, rinsed

250g cooked chickpeas

juice of ½ lemon

bunch of coriander, chopped

Heat the olive oil in a large, heavy-bottomed saucepan. Add the mutton cubes and brown slightly. Add the onions and celery and cook together with a little salt for several minutes until they are soft and just beginning to brown.

Add all the spices and the chopped parsley and season with salt and pepper. Cook for a minute or so before adding the tomatoes. Cook for 3–4 minutes stirring occasionally to break up the tomatoes. Pour over the water and bring to the boil. Turn down to a simmer and cook, uncovered, for about 1–1½ hours or until the mutton is tender.

Add the lentils and continue to cook for about 20 minutes. When the lentils are soft, add the cooked chickpeas. You may need to top up with a little water at this stage. Finally, add the lemon juice and chopped coriander, check the seasoning and serve.

SOUTHERN INDIAN STYLE MUTTON CURRY

Serves 6–8

2 tsp each cumin seeds, coriander seeds and fennel seeds
1 tsp each of mustard seeds and fenugreek seeds
1kg mutton shoulder, cut into 3cm chunks
salt and pepper
2 tbsp olive oil, plus extra for frying
300g shallots, sliced
3 garlic cloves, sliced
100g root ginger, peeled and diced
2 red chillies, halved, deseeded and finely sliced
400g tin of chopped tomatoes
8–10 curry leaves, dried or fresh
500ml water

First, toast the spices by placing them all in a dry frying pan over a medium heat. Leave them for less than a minute or until starting to crackle. Tip them into a pestle and mortar and grind them to a powder, then set them aside.

Season the pieces of mutton with salt and pepper. In a large casserole, heat the oil and brown the mutton pieces on all sides. Remove to a plate. Add some more oil to the pan if needed and fry the shallots, garlic and ginger for a few minutes until soft and starting to colour. Add the chilli and continue to cook for another minute.

Add the toasted spices to casserole and stir well. Pour in the tomatoes, add the curry leaves and cook for a few minutes until you have a thick, scented paste. Return the browned mutton pieces to the casserole and season well. Pour over 500ml water and bring to the boil. Turn down to a gentle simmer and cover with a piece of baking parchment and a lid.

Cook slowly for 1–1½ hours or until the meat is tender and the sauce has thickened. Traditionally this is served with rice or flatbread.

TOMATO

TOMATO
with RECIPES *by* GARY RHODES

Think of bite-sized sweet little cherry tomatoes and fleshy fragrant plum tomatoes still clinging to the vine. There are tiger tomatoes with stripes and some that are green, and even tomatoes the size of grapefruits called Oxheart. This wonderful, fleshy, juicy fruit is the ruby jewel in our British food heritage crown.

First cultivated for their decorative appearance in the eighteenth century, it was more than a century later that Britain began to grow this delicious fruit on a grand scale. But demand has now outstripped supply and 80% of the tomatoes eaten in the UK are now imported. It has become increasingly hard for British farmers to compete with desert-grown imports; a problem compounded by the fact that the price paid per kilo has barely risen in recent years.

With only 40 commercial growers left in Britain, is it really worth saving the humble home-grown tomato? Many believe that the tomatoes we produce have a superior flavour to imported varieties. A domestically grown fruit can make it from vine to shelf in as few as 24 hours. This means the tomato can be left to ripen on the plant for longer, making for a sweeter flesh and a more full-flavoured fruit.

Thankfully many British growers are rising to the challenge and are taking on the imports in the battle for our shelves, as well as keeping abreast of current trends so vital to meeting the demands and tastes of the public. For example, vine tomatoes now account for over half the UK's production area. In addition, the British growing season is surprisingly long, lasting from February to the end of October, with the seasonal peak during in May. During this period, we should all be buying British and treating ourselves to a richer, more satisfying fruit.

Britain's tomato growers have made encouraging developments. They have increased yields by harnessing eco-friendly forms of energy to power their greenhouses, to increase their harvest threefold.

We have the best tomatoes in the world but the growers need our help. Choose British for a deeper, sweeter flavour. From a simple tomato salad to a rich, deep pasta sauce, the rewards of buying locally will be evident in the delicious food you enjoy.

ENGLISH MOZZARELLA, TOMATO *and* BASIL SALAD

The cherry tomatoes in this recipe are semi-dried, which increases their already powerful flavour. As the tomatoes dry, the juices are absorbed by the flesh and become richer as time passes. *Gary Rhodes*

Serves 2

Oven-dried tomato confit
200g cherry tomatoes, halved
1 garlic clove, crushed
2 sprigs of thyme, picked
25ml olive oil
pinch of sea salt
freshly milled black pepper
10g icing sugar

Fresh tomato vinaigrette
2 'bottled' sun-dried tomatoes
 (4 halves), roughly chopped
10 fresh ripe cherry tomatoes,
 quartered

1 tsp smooth Dijon mustard
2 tsp red wine vinegar
 (Cabernet Sauvignon)
salt and pepper
pinch of sugar
2 tbsp olive oil
1 tbsp sesame oil

Salad
120g mozzarella (approximately 1 ball)
basil and baby cress leaves, to garnish

Preheat the oven to 85°C/19°F/Gas ¼. For the confit, line a baking tray with a piece of greaseproof paper. Place the halved cherry tomatoes in a bowl along with the rest of the ingredients (except the icing sugar) and mix well. Then put the tomato halves on the lined baking tray, dust with icing sugar and place in the oven for about 25–35 minutes.

For the vinaigrette, place the chopped bottled tomatoes and quartered cherry tomatoes in a food processor and blitz at high speed to liquidise. Rest a sieve over a bowl and scrape the tomato purée into it. Push the pulp through, until only the pips and skin are left.

In a second bowl, dissolve the mustard in the vinegar with a pinch of salt and the sugar. Season with black pepper, then whisk in the olive and sesame oils in a gradual trickle. Then whisk the vinaigrette into the sieved tomato.

On a plate arrange the sliced mozzarella, oven-dried tomatoes and drizzle with the tomato vinaigrette. Garnish with basil leaves and baby cress.

PAN-FRIED SALMON
with TOMATOES, SHRIMPS *and* FRESH HERBS

With this salmon recipe, I love to add lots and lots of fresh chopped tomatoes to the olive oil and shrimps, which help add a sweet bite with a slight sharpness to complete the vinaigrette. *Gary Rhodes*

Serves 3

Tomato and shrimp sauce
15ml olive oil
25g brown shrimps, peeled
1–2 plum or salad tomatoes,
    blanched, peeled and diced
mixed bunch of parsley,
    tarragon, chives, chervil,
    chopped
sea salt and pepper

Spinach
knob of butter
generous handful of spinach leaves,
    picked and washed

Salmon
salt and pepper
3 x 50g square fillets of salmon, skinned
15ml olive oil
squeeze of lemon juice

To make the sauce, warm the oil in a pan but do not let it become too hot. Add the shrimps and gently warm. Add the tomatoes and finally the herbs. Season to taste.

Melt the butter in another frying or saucepan. Once sizzling add the spinach leaves, stirring for just a minute or two until the leaves are tender. Season with salt and pepper and drain. The leaves can be spooned onto a plate lined with a clean J-Cloth. This will help soak up any excess water remaining in the leaves.

Season and fry the salmon fillets in a hot pan with a little olive oil, allowing them to colour on one side before turning the fillets and repeating the process. The fillets will only take 3–4 minutes in total, keeping a succulent moist centre. Finish with a squeeze of lemon juice.

Divide the leaves into three piles on a main course serving plate. Top each with a fillet of the fish, spooning the tomato, shrimp and fresh herb sauce on top of each and serve.

ALMOND PUDDING
with LIME SYRUP *and*
ENGLISH WHITE TOMATO SORBET

The sorbet is made with sugar, liquid glucose and tomato water – not juice. Liquidise the tomatoes quickly, leaving chunks still with texture. Once drained, which is best done overnight through a muslin, the juices will be clear and, when churned, the mix is almost brilliant white in colour, but tastes of the richest and sweetest red fruit around. *Gary Rhodes*

Serves 4

White tomato sorbet
100g liquid glucose
100g caster sugar
500ml white tomato juice

Almond pudding
320g unsalted butter,
  room temperature
120g caster sugar
125g good-quality ground almonds

1 level tsp baking powder
25g plain flour
25g crumbled digestive biscuits
3 free range eggs

Lime syrup
100ml lime juice
  (approximately 3–4 limes)
50g caster sugar
splash of vanilla essence or 1 vanilla pod,
  (optional)

You will need an ice cream machine and four 10cm loose-bottom tart tins.

Pre-chill the ice cream machine. Meanwhile, heat the glucose, sugar and tomato juice together until the sugar has dissolved. Boil together for a few minutes before straining and leaving to cool. Then churn in the ice cream machine.

Preheat the oven to 140°C/275°F/Gas 1. Line the tart tins twice with soft butter then flour and set aside. Place all of the ingredients for the almond pudding in a food processor and blitz until smooth.

Divide between the four greased tart tins and cook for 15–19 minutes, until they start to come away from the sides and are firm to the touch. Remove from the oven to cool.

For the lime syrup, gently warm the lime juice and the caster sugar together until the sugar has dissolved. The syrup is now ready to drizzle over each of the almond puddings. A splash of vanilla essence or one vanilla pod can be added to the syrup for extra flavour.

When the almond puddings have been allowed to cool, place each on a large bowl or plate. Drizzle with the syrup and top with a scoop of the sorbet.

ROAST TOMATO TART

Serves 4

Pastry
200g plain flour
100g butter, very cold and cut
   into small pieces
pinch of salt
60ml ice-cold water

Filling
500g vine tomatoes, halved
2 garlic cloves, crushed to a paste with salt
small bunch thyme, leaves stripped
   and stems discarded
2 tbsp olive oil
salt and pepper
200g mascarpone cheese
200g Gruyère cheese, grated
1 tsp Dijon mustard
4 free range eggs, beaten

To make the pastry, put the flour, butter and salt into a food processor and blitz for a couple of seconds. The butter will be mixed in but still in little chunks, slightly coarser than breadcrumbs. Pour into a bowl and add the cold water. Using a fork, mix the water through the flour then bring it together into a ball with your hands. Cover with Cling film and refrigerate for 1 hour.

Meanwhile, preheat the oven to 200°C/400°F/Gas 6. Put the halved tomatoes into a roasting tray. In a small bowl or jug mix the crushed garlic, thyme leaves, olive oil and salt and pepper. Pour this over the tomatoes and toss them to coat. Place the tray in the hot oven. After 20 minutes remove the tomatoes from the oven and set them aside. Turn the oven down to 180°C/350°F/Gas 4.

Once the pastry has rested, unwrap it and set it on a lightly floured surface. Roll it out into a circle large enough to cover a 23cm tart tin. Set the pastry into the tin pressing it gently into the sides and pierce some holes in the base with a fork to allow air to escape as it cooks. Bake blind for 15–20 minutes or until light golden. Remove and turn the oven down to 170°C/325°F/Gas 3.

In a bowl, mix the mascarpone cheese, Gruyère cheese and mustard. Add the eggs and mix well. Season to taste with salt and pepper. Pour the mixture into the tart shell and arrange the roasted tomatoes on top. Set on an oven tray and bake for 30–35 minutes or until firm to the touch.

GAZPACHO

Serves 2–4   1kg ripe red tomatoes, halved
1 green pepper, deseeded and roughly chopped
1 cucumber, peeled, deseeded and roughly chopped
2 shallots, grated
3 slices of stale sourdough or white bread, crumbled into small pieces
2 garlic cloves, crushed to a paste with salt
1 tbsp good-quality red wine vinegar
1 tbsp extra virgin olive oil
sea salt and pepper

Blend the tomatoes, green pepper and cucumber together to a smooth pulp. Add the grated shallots, bread and garlic and mix.

Sieve about one-third of the mixture into a bowl, using a ladle to push the pulp through the sieve to extract the maximum liquid. Discard the contents of the sieve then add the other two-thirds of the blended pulp to the bowl. You will have a semi-smooth liquid measuring about 1 litre.

Add the red wine vinegar and olive oil and season well with salt and pepper. Cover and refrigerate for at least an hour, then taste and adjust the flavour if necessary with more vinegar or seasoning. Serve very cold with extra ice, if you like, or in pre-chilled bowls or glasses.

THREE TOMATO SAUCES
for PASTA

COOKED TOMATO SAUCE

Serves 4–6   90ml olive oil
            1 red onion, sliced
            1kg large ripe tomatoes, such as beefsteak, cut into chunks
            1 tbsp good-quality dried oregano
            salt and pepper

Heat 2 tbsp of the oil in a large saucepan and fry the onion until it is soft and sweet and just starting to colour. Add the tomatoes and the oregano and season well with salt and pepper. Cover and cook gently for 10 minutes. Uncover and stir well and continue to cook, stirring from time to time, for another 30 minutes or until you have a thick sauce.

Remove from the heat, stir through the rest of the olive oil and blend to a purée. Pass this through a sieve or a mouli-legume, if you have one, to create a smooth sauce.

ROASTED TOMATO SAUCE

Serves 4–6   1kg plum tomatoes
            2 garlic cloves, crushed to a paste with salt
            4 sprigs of thyme, leaves stripped and stems discarded
            90ml olive oil
            salt and pepper

Preheat the oven to 180°C/350°F/Gas 4. In a large bowl, mix the tomatoes with the garlic paste, thyme leaves and olive oil. Season well with salt and pepper and lay on an oven tray.

Roast for 35–40 minutes. The tomatoes will have become slightly smaller and darker with a wonderfully intense flavour. Toss them and any juices with cooked pasta to serve.

RAW TOMATO SAUCE
with CAPERS

Serves 4–6   500g cherry tomatoes, halved or quartered
20g capers, roughly chopped
4 sprigs of fresh marjoram, leaves picked and roughly chopped,
   stems discarded
salt and pepper
1 tbsp good-quality red wine vinegar
60ml extra virgin olive oil

Place the chopped tomatoes in a large bowl. Stir in the chopped capers and marjoram leaves. Season well with the salt and pepper and the vinegar. Stir in the olive oil.

FRIED GREEN TOMATOES

Serves 6
as a snack

1 free range egg, beaten
salt and pepper
4 tbsp coarse polenta
3 green tomatoes, sliced into 2cm thick discs
3 tbsp olive oil

Line a plate with kitchen paper and set aside. Put the beaten egg into a medium-sized bowl and season well with salt and pepper. Pour the polenta onto a large plate. Take a green tomato slice and dip it into the egg, then turn it over in the polenta to coat completely.

Heat the olive oil in a frying pan until it is smoking. Place the coated tomato slices in the oil and brown until they become crisp. Carefully turn them over and repeat on the other side. Remove to the lined plate. Sprinkle with extra salt to serve.

GREEN TOMATO CHUTNEY

Makes
about 3 x
200ml jars

1kg green tomatoes, quartered
400g cooking apples, peeled, cored and cut into pieces
300g shallots, sliced
100g sultanas
250g demerara sugar
250ml malt vinegar
2 tsp mustard seed
2 tsp salt
20g root ginger, peeled and sliced
5 green chillies, cut in half lengthways

You will need a 10cm square piece of muslin, some kitchen string and three sterilised 200ml jars with tightly fitting lids.

Put all the ingredients except the ginger and chillies into a large, heavy-bottomed saucepan. Wrap the ginger and chilli in the muslin and tie firmly. Add this to the rest of the ingredients.

Bring to the boil and then turn down to a simmer and cook very gently for 2 hours. Stir occasionally so that the mixture doesn't stick on the bottom.

After 2 hours, check the consistency. It should be a little chunky still but thick and dark. Taste and add more salt if necessary.

To sterilise the jars, wash and dry them thoroughly then heat them in an oven set at 150°C/300°F/Gas 2 for 10 minutes.

Remove the muslin bundle from the saucepan and discard. Spoon the chutney into the jars and seal immediately.

PANZANELLA

Serves 4–6   300g white ciabatta, crusts removed
200g ripe tomatoes
1 cucumber, peeled, seeds removed
¼ red onion, finely sliced
2 tbsp good-quality red wine vinegar
8 tbsp extra virgin olive oil
salt and pepper
1 large bunch of basil, leaves picked from the stalks

Tear the ciabatta into 4cm chunks. Toast under the grill for a couple of minutes so it is dry on the outside and toasted but still a little soft within.

Cut the tomatoes in half and then into rough chunks, similar to the size of the bread. Slice the cucumber at an angle into thick pieces. In a bowl, mix the bread, tomato and onion. Pour over the vinegar and 6 tbsp of the oil and season well with salt and pepper. Mix well then leave to infuse for at least 15 minutes.

When you are ready to eat, add the cucumber, then roughly chop the basil leaves and mix into the salad. Pour over the remaining oil to serve.

APPLE

APPLE
with RECIPES *by* JAMES MARTIN

One of the great fruits of Britain is the apple. Apple trees grow all over the countryside, both wild and cultivated. Even in cities, during the late summer and autumn you see trees laden with the beautiful fruit. This makes it hard to understand why the apple needs reviving, particularly with every supermarket offering them year round in abundance. The truth is that up to 65% of the apples on the shelves during the British season are foreign imports and this isn't because we don't grow enough to supply such huge demand. Supermarkets and shops choose to import varieties from France or even as far away as New Zealand to take their place.

There are plenty of fantastic British apple varieties but most of us would have trouble naming just a few. You might know Cox and Bramley but how about Feltham Beauty, Blenheim Orange and Discovery? Each apple variety has its own unique characteristics, from the subtle nutty, almost dry texture of the Egremont Russet to the deliciously sweet and floral flavour of Worcester Pearmain via the intriguing, sharp and tangy Crispin. These great British apples are under threat.

More than a thousand varieties of native apples used to be grown in the UK. Now as few as eight are commercially available. It's true to say that tastes have changed over the years and today people prefer a bigger, juicier and sweeter apple. Large retailers also have strict requirements: a small apple, or one with blemishes, may well taste delicious but it simply isn't considered to be commercially viable.

It's no surprise then that we've lost 60% of our orchards since the 1950s and now have just 500 commercial apple growers compared with 1,525 some years ago. Such stringent standardisation often means that while we may end up with great-looking apples, many are severely lacking in true flavour and sweetness.

Seasonality has always been with us but we have grown accustomed to uniform produce being available all-year-round. Many British apples can be happily stored for up to nine months so why only in the early stages of autumn do we see our native apples available?

It's down to us to pay attention when we're buying apples. Read the labels and buy British whenever possible and if you're struggling to find what you're after, contact local growers because many sell through markets, farmer's markets and even directly to your door. With greater demand comes greater availability. Whether it's a crunchy sweet toffee apple or an elegant tarte tatin, rediscover the fun of cooking Britain's most delicious fruit.

SLOW ROAST BELLY OF PORK
with SPICED APPLE *and* CIDER SAUCE *and* MASHED POTATOES

Pork belly has a nice mix of fat and meat so it is perfect to roast. The difference is, to get a good crackling, I pop the pork into a hot oven first for 30–45 minutes and then turn the temperature down and slow roast for 2½ to 3 hours. The perfect accompaniment to this dish is apple sauce, which has been served with fatty meats for thousands of years. Most importantly, don't over sugar the apples in the sauce: you need that sharpness for the sauce to work. And it's so easy to make there is no excuse to buy ready-made stuff! *James Martin*

Serves 4–6

Pork
1.3kg pork belly, boned
salt and pepper
10 sage leaves, 6 whole and 4 chopped
1 Bramley apple, peeled, cored and
    finely grated
3 onions, sliced
splash of artisan cider, medium sweet

Apple sauce
500g Bramley apples, peeled,
    cored and cut into chunks
30g butter
2 tbsp water

2 tbsp artisan cider, medium sweet
¼ tsp nutmeg, freshly grated
¼ ground cinnamon
¼ tsp black pepper
30g soft dark brown sugar

Mash
900g Maris Piper potatoes,
    peeled and quartered
120ml double cream
100g unsalted butter, cubed
salt and pepper
nutmeg, freshly grated

Preheat the oven to 230°C/450°F/Gas 4. Score the pork belly skin with a sharp knife, making scores 1cm apart. Place the belly skin-side down, season with salt and freshly ground black pepper. Place the six whole sage leaves and the grated apple on to the meat. Roll up the belly and secure with string. Arrange the onion in the bottom of a roasting tray and scatter over the chopped sage leaves. Splash in some cider, place the meat on top and put in the oven. After 20 minutes, turn the oven down to 150°C/300°F/Gas 2 and leave to roast for a further 3 hours. Once it is cooked and tender, remove from the oven and leave to rest for 10 minutes.

Meanwhile, put the apple chunks into a saucepan with the butter, water, cider and spices. Cover the pan and cook over a medium heat until the apples are soft enough to beat into a purée. Add the sugar and stir through. Taste, and add more sugar if necessary. Set aside until you are ready to serve.

About 40–45 minutes before the pork has finished, make the mash. Place the potatoes in cold salted water and bring to the boil and cook for 20 minutes until tender, then drain. Put a lid on the saucepan and shake vigorously to break up the potatoes. Gradually add the cream and butter while mashing the potatoes. Season to taste with salt, freshly ground black pepper and freshly grated nutmeg. Serve with slices of roast pork and apple sauce.

APPLE CHARLOTTE
with THYME CUSTARD

There are two main types of Charlotte desserts – one hot and one cold. The cold one is normally a mousse base set with gelatine and lined with sponge fingers, while the hot one is lined with bread and baked. This is the hot version and is best cooked and served straight away. If reheated the bread gets too hard and the inside can become dry. This is a dish that lends itself best to apples that are slightly sharply flavoured to the taste. *James Martin*

Serves 6

Charlottes
6 Braeburn apples, peeled,
    cored and roughly chopped
60g caster sugar
½ tbsp lemon juice
3 tbsp water
150g butter
2 Braeburn apples, peeled, cored and
    thinly sliced
10 slices bread, crusts removed

Custard
6 free range egg yolks
75g caster sugar
200ml whole milk
200ml double cream
2 sprigs of thyme

Preheat the oven to 180°C/350°F/Gas 4. Place the roughly chopped apples, sugar, lemon juice and water into a saucepan along with 25g of the butter. Bring to the boil, then reduce the heat and simmer until tender.

Melt the remaining butter in a pan and, with a pastry brush, butter six ramekins. Arrange the thinly sliced apples like a fan at the bottom of each ramekin. When turned out, these will form the top of the Charlotte.

Cut the slices of bread in half, then into four slices like fingers. Dip each bread finger in the remaining melted butter and place around the side of each ramekin, leaving no gaps. Keep some fingers back for the lid. Spoon the apple mix into the ramekins, pressing it down well. Top with the remaining bread. Place in the oven for 25 minutes.

Meanwhile, make the custard by whisking the egg yolks and sugar in a bowl. Heat the milk, cream and thyme in a non-stick pan until it is at scalding point. Pour the milk mixture onto the egg yolks slowly, whisking the whole time.

Pour the mixture back into the pan and heat gently, stirring all the time, until the mixture is thick enough to coat the back of a spoon. Pass mixture through a fine sieve into a bowl. When the charlottes are ready, turn them out onto individual serving plates and spoon some hot custard over each to serve.

APPLE, CUSTARD *and* HONEY TART

This is a great way to use two types of flavour from apples in one dessert. It is best to use a cooking type of apple for the base of the tart and an eating apple as the cooked garnish. When cooking the tart in the oven with the custard inside, keep it at a low temperature or the mixture will soufflé and curdle. Also, I like to serve custard-based desserts at room temperature because the flavour and texture are better than straight from the fridge. *James Martin*

Serves 4–6

Pastry
225g plain flour
50g caster sugar
1 vanilla pod, seeds scraped out
125g unsalted butter, slightly softened
1 medium free range egg,
    lightly beaten
1 medium free range egg yolk

Filling
1 large Bramley apple, peeled,
    cored and roughly sliced
1 tbsp water
caster sugar, to taste
4 Cox apples, peeled,
    cored and neatly sliced
20g unsalted butter

3 medium free range egg yolks
2 medium free range eggs
1 tbsp clear honey
600ml double cream

Topping
25g butter
1 small red eating apple, Ballard
    Beauty if available, cored
    and cut into 1cm slices
icing sugar, to taste
½ tsp ground nutmeg
1 cinnamon stick
½ tsp ground star anise
¼ tsp ground cloves
splash of brandy
double cream, to serve

You will need at 23cm loose-bottomed tart tin.

Set the oven to 180°C/350°F/Gas 4, and place a baking sheet in the oven, on the middle shelf, to preheat. Rub the flour, sugar, vanilla seeds and butter together gently with your fingertips until they resemble breadcrumbs (or pulse in a food processor). Pour the beaten egg onto the mixture and stir it in with a spoon. Bring everything together with your hands to form a dough. Place in a bowl, cover with Cling film and rest in the fridge for 30 minutes.

Lightly grease the tart tin. Roll out the pastry into a circle 3mm thick and 23cm wide. Gently ease the pastry into the tin, pressing down so there are no air bubbles. Leave 2.5cm of the pastry overhanging the edge. Chill for 10 minutes.

Take the pastry case out of the fridge, line with greaseproof paper and fill with dried beans or rice. Put the pastry case onto the preheated baking sheet and bake for 8 minutes. Remove from the oven and carefully lift off the paper with the beans or rice. Bake the pastry case in the oven for a further 5 minutes, until the pastry no longer looks glassy.

Carefully trim off the overhanging pastry edge level with the top of the tin, and then brush the inside of the case with the egg yolk to seal the pastry. Put the pastry case back into the oven for a further 3 minutes to cook the yolk, then remove from the oven and set aside.

Reduce the oven temperature to 170°C/325°F/Gas 3. To make the filling, place the Bramley apple slices in a saucepan with 1 tbsp water. Cook over a medium heat for 5–10 minutes, until soft. Sweeten with sugar to taste and beat to a purée, then pour into the bottom of the pastry case. Arrange the Golden Noble slices over the top of the purée.

In a bowl, beat together the egg yolks, whole eggs and honey. Place the cream in a small pan and bring to the boil. When boiling, whisk the cream into the egg mix, beating all the time. Pour over the sliced apples in the pastry case. Place in the oven and bake for 20 minutes, until the mixture has set and is golden brown.

To make the topping, heat a non-stick pan over a medium heat, and add the butter. Once the butter begins to bubble add the Ballard Beauty apple slices, the spices and a little sugar. Allow it to cook for 2 minutes until it begins to caramelise, then add a splash of brandy. Remove from the heat and serve alongside a wedge of the tart and with a dollop of cream.

PHEASANT
BRAISED *with* CIDER *and* APPLES

Serves 4
2 large pheasants, weighing about 1.5kg in total
salt and pepper
2 tbsp olive oil
100g smoked streaky bacon, cut into 1cm strips
100g shallots, sliced
small bunch of thyme, leaves stripped and stems discarded
8 juniper berries
1 litre cider
500ml chicken stock
150ml crème fraiche
25g butter
4 Cox apples, peeled, cored and cut into eighths
juice of 1 lemon

First joint the pheasants. Put the bird on its back on a carving board and gently pull a leg away from the body. Slip the knife between the leg and body and cut through the skin. Bend the leg back to snap and release the joint and cut downwards to remove the leg from the body. Repeat on the other side.

To remove the breasts and wings together, keep the bird on its back, cut through the ribs to remove the under-cavity so that you are left with both breasts and wings on the bone. Using poultry shears or kitchen scissors, cut through the length of the breastbone so that you are left with two breasts on the bone with wing tips attached at each end.

Season the pheasant pieces. Heat 2 tbsp olive oil in a large casserole and brown the joints all over. Remove to a plate. Add the bacon to the casserole and fry until crisp. Then add the shallots and thyme leaves and cook to soften, about 2 minutes.

Return the pheasant to the pan along with the juniper berries and pour over the cider. Boil for a minute to cook off the alcohol and reduce the liquid slightly. Add the stock and season well. Reduce to a simmer, cover with a piece of baking parchment and cook gently for about 25 minutes.

Remove the pheasant breasts and keep warm; continue to cook the legs for 20 minutes. Then remove the legs and boil the liquid for several minutes to reduce by about half. Whisk in the crème fraiche and taste for seasoning. Keep warm until serving.

Meanwhile, in a large frying pan, melt the butter and fry the apple pieces. Resist the temptation to turn them too often, to allow them to brown well without breaking up. Stir the apples and the pheasant back into the sauce to serve. This is excellent accompanied by mashed celeriac.

APPLE MERINGUE PUDDING

Serves 4–6   50g butter
500g Bramley apples, peeled, cored and quartered
2cm cinnamon stick
4 cloves
220g caster sugar
2 free range egg whites
1 tsp cornflour

In a heavy-bottomed saucepan, melt the butter and add the apple, cinnamon, cloves and 100g of the sugar. Cover with a lid and cook on a low heat for about 15 minutes or until the apple has softened and is falling apart. Remove the cinnamon and cloves and discard. Blend the apple mixture to a smooth purée, spoon into a shallow baking dish and leave to cool.

Preheat the oven to 130°C/250°F/Gas ½. To make the meringue, whisk the egg whites until they start to bubble. Add 60g of the sugar and the cornflour and continue to whisk. Every time the consistency of the whites changes, add a little more sugar until all of it is incorporated. Continue whisking until the whites form stiff peaks. Spoon the whites over the top of the apple purée and bake for about 1–1¼ hours or until the meringue is firm and a little brown.

APPLE *and* PLUM CRUMBLE *with* ALMOND

Serves 6   300g Victoria plums, halved and stoned
1 vanilla pod, seeds scraped out
juice of 1 lemon
50g caster sugar
500g Cox or Royal Gala apples, peeled, cored and quartered

Crumble
75g cold, unsalted butter, cut into cubes
100g self-raising flour
75g demerara sugar
50g ground almonds

Preheat the oven to 200°C/400°F/Gas 6. Put the plums in a roasting dish and mix in the vanilla seeds, half of the lemon juice and the sugar. Bake for about 20 minutes until the plums are soft but not falling apart. Remove from the oven and set aside. Turn the oven down to 180°C/350°F/Gas 4.

Toss the apple quarters with the remaining lemon juice. Then stir the apple into the cooked plums and leave to cool.

Meanwhile, prepare the crumble. Chop the butter into the flour until it resembles fine crumbs. Stir in the sugar and the ground almonds until you have a mixture resembling damp sand. Refrigerate for at least 10 minutes.

Put the plum and apple mixture into a deep baking dish. Pour the crumble mixture evenly over the fruit and pat down lightly. Bake for at least 30 minutes or until the top is golden brown and crunchy and the juices from the fruit are bubbling up the sides of the dish.

TARTE TATIN

Serves 4   flour, for dusting
300g puff pastry
100g caster sugar
100g butter, cut into small pieces
600g apples, such as Cox, Bramley or Discovery, peeled and sliced into eighths

Preheat the oven to 190°C/375°F/Gas 5. On a lightly floured surface, roll the pastry into a disc 1cm thick and large enough to cover the top of the pan with a little extra to hang over the edge. Set the rolled pastry aside.

In a non-stick 25cm ovenproof frying pan, about 5cm deep, melt the sugar over a medium heat and when it starts to caramelise, add the pieces of butter one at a time. Continue cooking until all the butter has melted and you have a smooth, bubbling liquid.

Lay the apple slices in the pan, in an overlapping circular fan shape. Continue cooking for 2 minutes to brown the bottom of the apples in the caramel but do not to let them burn.

Remove the pan from the heat and lay the pastry over the top of the apples. Tuck any excess pastry around the apples and into the pan. Place the pan on a baking sheet and bake for 20–25 minutes or until the pastry is golden and crisp.

To serve, select a plate that fits snugly over the top of the pan. Hold the pan and plate firmly together and quickly flip the pan upside down on top of the plate. Carefully lift away the pan, leaving the tarte tatin apple-side up on the plate.

CRAB-APPLE *and* ROSEHIP JELLY

Makes	200g rosehips, washed well
enough	500g crab-apples, cleaned and cut roughly in half
to fill 3	juice of 1 lemon
standard	500g sugar, for every 600ml strained juice
jam jars	2 sprigs of rosemary

You will need a jelly bag or muslin cloth, three sterilised jam jars with tightly fitting lids and three discs of waxed paper that will fit inside the jar on top of the jelly.

Cook the rosehips and crab-apples separately as the rosehips take much longer than the apples. Either do this in two separate pots or one after the other.

Cover the whole rosehips with water in a saucepan and set over the heat to bring to the boil. Turn down to a simmer and cook gently until very soft, at least 40 minutes. You may need to top up the water during cooking.

Place the crab-apples in a bowl, pour over the lemon juice and toss to coat. Transfer to a saucepan, cover well with water and bring to the boil. Reduce the temperature and simmer until the apples are soft and falling apart, about 15 minutes.

Mix the cooked rosehips and apples and their cooking liquid together and gently mash them into a wet pulp. Pour this into a jelly bag or muslin cloth and strain overnight into a large bowl.

The next day, prepare your jars for sterilising. Preheat the oven to 150C/300°F/Gas 2. Wash and dry the jars thoroughly and place them upside down in the oven for 10 minutes. Put a saucer in the freezer to cool. (You will need this to test the setting point of the jelly.)

Measure the strained liquid and add 500g sugar for each 600ml of strained juice. Return to the pan and add the rosemary. Bring to the boil then reduce to a gentle simmer. Depending on how much liquid you have, you may want to start testing the setting point after just 5 minutes or so. This jelly naturally contains a lot of pectin, so it can reach the setting point quite quickly.

Take the saucer from the freezer and put a large drop of hot jelly onto it. Draw your finger through the middle of the liquid. If the parted liquid leaves a clear line where your finger has drawn, then it is ready. Remove the rosemary from the mixture and discard. Using a ladle, divide the jelly between the three prepared jars. Cover the jelly with a disc of waxed paper, screw on the lid and leave to cool.

SPICED HOT CIDER

Serves 4
1 litre British cider, dry or sweet
50ml British cider brandy
3 slivers of orange zest
1 cinnamon stick
5 cloves
5 allspice berries
4 tbsp honey
nutmeg, grated

Put all the ingredients together in a saucepan, grating in some fresh nutmeg. Bring the liquid to a simmer. Turn off the heat and leave to sit for 20 minutes to allow the flavours to infuse. When you are ready to serve, gently reheat and then strain into a serving jug. Drink hot, served in cups.

TOFFEE APPLES

Makes 6

oil, for greasing
6 small Russet apples, stalks removed
225g demerara sugar
110ml water
1 tsp good-quality white wine vinegar
1 tbsp golden syrup
30g butter
½ tsp vanilla essence

Lightly oil a baking tray and set it aside. Skewer each apple with a strong wooden stick, pushing it down through the core and set aside. Place the sugar and water together in a pan over a moderate heat. When the sugar has dissolved, add the vinegar, syrup and butter. Bring the mixture to the boil and boil rapidly for about 8–10 minutes until it reaches 140°C/275°F, known as the hard-crack stage in candy-making terms. Otherwise, a good way to test it is by putting a drop in a glass of cold water, if it hardens into a ball it is ready, if it is still soft and tacky, it needs to boil longer. Be careful not to burn the mixture or it will taste very bitter.

When it is ready, remove from the heat and stir in the vanilla. Holding the end of the stick, dip each apple into the toffee and twist around to cover it completely. Allow the excess to drip off before placing on the oiled tray with the stick pointing upwards, if possible, to cool and harden. They will be ready to eat in just a matter of minutes.

HONEY

HONEY
with RECIPES *by* AINSLEY HARRIOTT

Thick and sweet or clear and scented, honey is one of nature's true wonder foods. It is pure and naturally sweet, subtly floral and good for us too. It is packed full of vitamins, minerals and amino acids. No two honeys taste the same as each variety is fragranced by the flowers from which the bees have gathered pollen.

Britain is famous for its intensely scented heather honey and gentle, floral blossom honey, so why is 90% of Britain's honey imported from around the world? We consume 30,000 tonnes of honey a year so that's enough demand to support all of our producers and keep high-quality British honey on our shelves. The problem lies in the fact that there can be no honey without bees and recently they have faced an increasingly difficult battle against disease and diminishing habitats. Today there are 75% fewer beehives than there were 100 years ago but thankfully there are some high-profile initiatives to help reverse this trend. However, we as consumers need to help our British bees.

When browsing the shelves, make sure you choose a pure English, Scottish, Welsh or Northern Irish honey. If its provenance is not stated clearly, the honey may be a blend or a foreign single-flower variety. Local honey is worth seeking out for the flavour but also for the nutritional and health benefits. Many people swear by it as a natural defence against hay fever. Others use it, and its derivatives, to help them fight off colds and to boost their immune system.

With no two jars being the same, the possibilities for experimenting are almost endless. As a fantastic marinade for rich meats, in breads, cakes or puddings or even to drink as a soothing balm or to help you sleep, honey is a magical ingredient. Use a subtle, mild-flavoured honey, such as general wildflower, to add a sweet, natural hint to dishes or pick a full-impact urban or heather honey for dishes where you want to keep the flavour identifiable. Most importantly, make sure you check the label for provenance and then get cooking.

WARM BAKED GOAT CHEESE SALAD *with* SEEDLESS GRAPES *and* WILD HONEY

Wild honey is perfect for breakfast. I like it on toast, fresh fruit or mixed with Greek yoghurt. And when it comes to cooking, for a touch of sweetness, it's wonderful in sauces or dressings. In this recipe, my grape dressing with warm baked goat cheese sitting on top of peppery watercress and fresh pear salad comes alive with the sweet floral aromas of the honey. You can get some great tasting British goat cheese now, especially from Somerset. Make sure you buy yours with the rind on to protect it when they are baked and glazed. *Ainsley Harriott*

Serves 4

50g bag of watercress
1 firm ripe pear, quartered,
    cored and thinly sliced
1 tbsp olive oil
juice of ½ lemon
sea salt flakes
freshly ground black pepper

4 slices of goat cheese with rind,
    each about 4cm thick
4 tbsp wild honey
100g seedless grapes
    (use a mixture of green and red)
4 tiny sprigs of thyme

Preheat the oven to 200°C/400°F/Gas 6. Place the watercress in a bowl. Fold the pear slices into the watercress and then lightly dress with olive oil and lemon juice. Season to taste with salt and freshly ground black pepper and set aside.

Arrange the goat cheese on a baking sheet lined with baking parchment and place in the oven for 3–4 minutes just to warm through. Meanwhile, place the honey in a small pan with the grapes and cover with a lid. Bring to the boil and then immediately remove from the heat.

Preheat the grill and quickly glaze the goat cheese (or a blow torch works very well). Divide the watercress and pear salad in small high piles between four plates. Spoon the grapes and honey around the edge of each plate. Using a fish slice, arrange the goat cheese on top. Garnish with the thyme sprigs and serve at once.

HONEYED DUCK BREASTS
with POTATO RÖSTI *and* CREAMED CABBAGE *and* BACON

Honey and duck is a great food combination the Chinese have been using for years. Basting duck breasts with honey while they are roasting gives a wonderful flavour and caramelises the skin. Duck has such an excellent flavour, richness and succulence that we often see it as being a little extravagant, which is probably why most of us only eat it in restaurants. Yet it's so easy to cook at home and, with a little practice, it will be just like dining out. This recipe came about after I'd experimented with some store-cupboard ingredients and I hope you'll agree it's an absolute winner. I prefer to use Gressingham duck breast for flavour and size. *Ainsley Harriott*

Serves 4

Honey and clove sauce
4 tbsp clear honey
2 tbsp dark soy sauce
2 tbsp balsamic vinegar
2 tbsp light Muscovado sugar
2 tbsp tomato ketchup
1 tsp whole cloves
225ml beef stock
salt and pepper

Rösti
2 large floury potatoes, peeled
sea salt and pepper
2–3 tbsp clarified butter or duck fat
2–3 tbsp sunflower oil

Cabbage and bacon
1 small Savoy cabbage,
    outer leaves removed
25g butter
1 onion, finely sliced
4 slices of streaky bacon,
    cut into strips, or packet of pancetta
2 tbsp water
4–6 tbsp double cream
salt and pepper

Duck breasts
4 x 275g duck breasts
1 tbsp cracked black pepper
pinch of salt
1 tbsp clear honey

Preheat the oven to 200°C/400°F/Gas 6. To make the sauce, place the honey in a small pan with the soy, vinegar, sugar, ketchup, cloves and stock. Bring to the boil, then reduce the heat and fast simmer for 5 minutes or until the mixture is thick enough to coat the back of a spoon. Season to taste and pass through a sieve into a clean pan, discarding the cloves. Set aside until needed.

For the rösti, grate the potatoes coarsely into the centre of a clean tea towel. Fold the towel around the potato to form a ball and squeeze to remove as much water as possible. Open the cloth and season with black pepper then divide into four equal portions.

Heat a large frying pan over medium heat. Add 2 tbsp of butter or duck fat and sunflower oil. Place a metal ring inside the frying pan and carefully add the grated potato. Using the back of a spoon gently push down to make a compact cake. Lift up the ring and repeat until you have four röstis.

Fry until golden brown, making sure that the fat bubbles up through the centre to cook the inside. Do not use too high a heat or the outside will burn before the centre is cooked. When golden, turn over and add the remaining oil, if required. Once golden brown, season with salt, then lift out of the pan and drain on kitchen paper. Place on a baking tray (they will keep for 4–5 hours) and reheat in a hot oven for 5 minutes when needed.

Cut the Savoy cabbage into quarters and remove the stalk. Finely slice the leaves, wash them and set aside. Melt the butter in the frying pan, add the onions and cook on medium heat for 4–5 minutes until softened.

Fry the bacon in a separate pan on a high heat until crisp and drain on kitchen paper. Season to taste with salt and white pepper, and keep warm until ready to serve, preferably when the duck is in the oven.

Score the fat on the duck in a criss-cross pattern and rub salt and pepper into the duck fat. Place duck breasts in a dry large ovenproof frying pan, skin-side down, allow the pan to heat up for three minutes until the fat starts to sizzle, giving the duck a crispy skin.

Turn the duck breasts over and cook for another minute, then pour away any excess fat. Pop them into the oven to cook for about 8–10 minutes for a pink finish. (You can leave them in the oven for a little longer if you prefer them well done). For the last few minutes of the cooking time brush the skin of the duck breasts with the honey. Leave to rest in a warm place for 5 minutes, without covering.

Add the cabbage and water to the onions and stir-fry over high heat for a few minutes until just tender. Add the crispy bacon and cream, stir to combine and simmer gently until the cream has slightly thickened. Reheat the rösti in the oven for 5 minutes while reheating the honey and clove sauce, stirring occasionally. Carve the duck breasts into thin slices and arrange on warmed plates with the rösti and Savoy cabbage, then drizzle around the honey and clove sauce to serve *(see p184)*.

CARAMELISED FIG *and* CHESTNUT HONEY TART

Philosophers and poets have praised the fig for centuries. It is perhaps the most sensual of fruits and has an exotic voluptuousness. The entire fruit is edible (the tiny seeds inside are in fact tiny fruits) but they're also perishable and will only last for about 3 days in the fridge, though they're never around for that long in my house! If you are eating them fresh make sure you take them out of the fridge well beforehand to really experience their delicate flavour. In this recipe (an idea from a delicious dessert I had in Italy) they're baked in an almond base tart with a gorgeous honey, orange and butter syrup. *Ainsley Harriott*

Serves 6

Pastry
250g plain flour,
   plus extra for dusting
125g unsalted butter, chilled
   cut into small pieces
4 tbsp icing sugar, sifted
2 free range eggs, beaten
baking beans, to weigh pastry base,
(optional)

Filling
50g ground almonds
6 ripe figs
3 tbsp chestnut honey
25g unsalted butter
1 tbsp fresh orange juice
50ml orange liqueur
crème fraiche, to serve
orange zest, grated, for garnish

To make the pastry, put the flour, butter and icing sugar into a food processor and blend together until the mixture looks like breadcrumbs. Add half the beaten egg and pulse briefly until the mixture just starts to stick together into a ball. If too sticky then add a little bit more flour. Turn out onto a lightly floured work surface and knead very briefly until smooth. Wrap in Cling film and chill for at least 20 minutes. (Two hours is best.)

Preheat the oven to 180°C/Gas 4. Roll out the pastry on a lightly floured board and use to line the six 10cm loose-bottomed tart tins. Prick the tart base with a fork and bake blind for 10–12 minutes. Remove the baking beans, brush with the remaining beaten egg and return to the oven for another 5–6 minutes until cooked through and lightly golden. Remove from the oven and leave to cool.

Melt the honey, butter, orange juice and liquor in a small pan and set aside.

Equally divide the ground almond into each of the pastry cases. From the top of the figs carefully cut two-thirds of the way through into 6 wedges then gently squeeze the base so they open like a flower. Arrange the figs in the pastry case and liberally brush with the honey butter and orange glaze.

Return the tarts to the oven for another 8–10 minutes, then remove and brush over with the remaining glaze. Serve on plates with a dollop of crème fraiche – sprinkle with the optional orange zest for garnish.

THE HAMILL'S
HONEY NUT BISCUITS

Here is a Hamill family recipe. The Hamills are third-generation beekeepers and owners of the Hive Honey Shop in London.

Makes 25
100g brown sugar
50ml dark honey, strained
100g shortening
50ml buttermilk
½ tsp baking soda, dissolved in 10ml hot water
280g white flour, sifted with 1 tsp baking powder
½ tsp salt
125g quick-cooking cereal oats
1 free range egg, beaten
75g mixed walnuts, hazelnuts and almonds, finely chopped
75g seedless raisins
1 tsp vanilla essence,
icing sugar, for dusting

Preheat the oven to 170°C/325°F/Gas 3. In a large mixing bowl, mix the ingredients in the order given into a batter, which should be about the same consistency as biscuit dough. Drop by spoonfuls, about the size of a walnut, onto a greased baking sheet. Bake for 15 minutes until golden brown. Once removed from the oven dust lightly with icing sugar and leave to cool on a wire rack.

HONEY ROAST HAM

Serves 4–6

2kg unsmoked boneless
   gammon joint
500ml cider
1 leek, trimmed and chopped
1 onion and 1 carrot, chopped
1 cinnamon stick
1 tsp each black peppercorns,
   coriander seeds and cloves

2 bay leaves
30 cloves, for studding

Glaze
200g demerara sugar
25ml sherry vinegar
100ml Madeira
250g honey

Put the gammon in a large pan and pour over the cider. Top up with cold water to cover. Add the leek, onion and carrot along with the spices and bay leaves. Bring to the boil, then turn it down to a simmer. Scoop off any scum that rises to the surface. If necessary, top up with a little more cold water. Simmer gently for about 2–2 ½ hours.

Preheat the oven to 200°C/400°F/Gas 6. Carefully remove the ham from the liquid and set aside to cool. (You can strain the leftover liquid and use it as ham stock for making soup or adding to pork dishes.)

When the ham is cool enough to handle, carefully slice off the skin, leaving a good layer of fat on the gammon. Make incisions in the fat in the traditional criss-cross pattern and stud it with the cloves. Put the ham into a roasting tin.

In a separate saucepan, dissolve the sugar in the vinegar and Madeira and bring to the boil. Add the honey and stir together well. Pour half of this over the ham and put it into the oven for about 20 minutes.

Remove the gammon from the oven and pour a little more of the glaze mixture over it. Repeat this a couple of times over the next 30 minutes, scooping any glaze from the bottom of the pan and spooning it back over the ham.

When the top of the ham looks brown and sticky, remove from the oven and leave it to rest for a few minutes. This can be eaten hot or left to cool and served later.

DEEP-FRIED AUBERGINES
with HONEY

Serves 4–6
as tapas

125g plain flour
1 free range egg, beaten
250ml cold water
½ tsp salt, plus extra to serve
1 litre sunflower oil, for frying
1 aubergine, sliced into 1cm slices
60–75ml runny honey, to serve

Sift the flour into a bowl. Make a well in the centre and pour in the egg. Slowly whisk from the centre outwards to mix it in. In a steady stream, pour in the cold water, stirring constantly with the whisk until all the liquid is incorporated and you have a smooth batter. Season with salt and set aside for 15 minutes.

Line a plate with some kitchen paper and set aside. Heat the oil in a large deep frying pan to 180°C/350°F. Dip the aubergine slices into the batter and fry them in small batches for a couple of minutes or until the outside is golden brown and crisp. Lift out of the pan using a slotted spoon and drain on the kitchen paper. To serve, drizzle over the honey and sprinkle with salt. Serve immediately.

HONEY, WALNUT *and* PECAN CAKE

Serves 6–8   200g butter, softened
100g caster sugar
3 free range eggs
4 tbsp set honey
200g self-raising flour, sifted
50g walnuts, roughly chopped
50g pecan nuts, roughly chopped
2 tbsp milk

Preheat the oven to 160°C/325°F/Gas 3. Use a little of the butter to grease a loaf tin approximately 20 x 8cm or a springform loose-bottomed cake tin and then line with baking parchment and set aside.

Beat the butter together with the sugar for 3–4 minutes until light and fluffy. Continue to beat and add the eggs, one by one, incorporating each egg thoroughly before you add the next.

Beat in the honey, then gently fold in the flour. Fold in the chopped nuts and loosen the mixture slightly with the milk. Spoon into the prepared tin and bake on the middle shelf of the oven for 35–40 minutes or until a skewer inserted into the centre comes out clean. Leave the cake to cool slightly on a wire rack before turning out and serving.

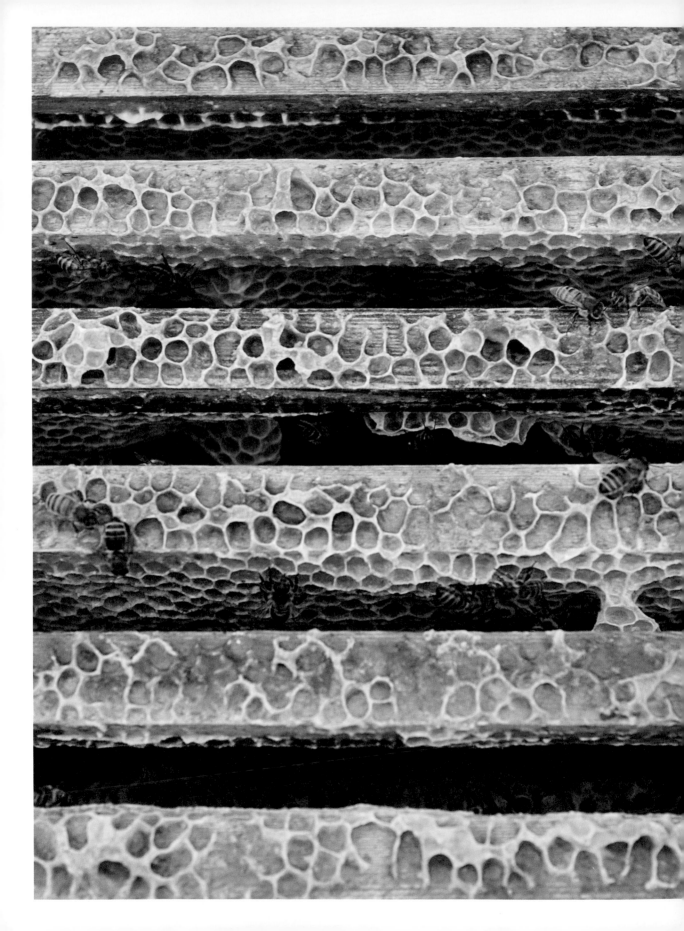

HONEY ICE CREAM
with HONEYCOMB

Serves 6–8

Honey ice cream
450ml double cream
150ml full fat milk
1 vanilla pod, seeds scraped out
5 free range egg yolks
3 tbsp set or runny honey

Honeycomb
10g butter
50g caster sugar
2 tbsp golden syrup
½ tbsp bicarbonate of soda

Put the cream and milk into a saucepan with the vanilla seeds. Heat until it is just starting to simmer. Remove and set aside. In a large bowl, whisk the egg yolks with the honey for a couple of minutes until pale and creamy. Slowly pour the heated cream in a steady stream onto the yolk mixture, whisking all the time. (Incorporating extra air like this will make a lighter, fluffier ice cream.) Pour into a shallow container to cool.

To make the honeycomb, grease a shallow metal tray with the butter and set aside. Place the sugar and syrup in a saucepan over a medium heat. When it has melted, increase the heat and cook for a couple of minutes or until it starts to darken and caramelise.

Remove from the heat and add the bicarbonate of soda. Whisk well while it fizzes to incorporate all the powder, then pour into the greased metal tray. Set in a cool place to harden, which takes only a couple of minutes. When it has hardened and cooled slightly, put both the ice cream mix and the honeycomb into the freezer.

Every 15 minutes or so, give the ice cream a whisk or a stir to break up the ice crystals as it freezes. When the ice cream is nearly solid, remove the honeycomb from the freezer, shatter it into small pieces and stir it through the ice cream. Return to the freezer to freeze completely. This will keep happily for up to a week in the freezer but is best eaten in the first couple of days.

GREEK HONEY BALLS

Makes 15–20 7g packet of dried yeast
200ml tepid water
350g plain flour
100g sugar
1 free range egg, beaten
50ml full fat milk, warmed
2 pinches of ground cinnamon
1 litre sunflower oil
3 tbsp aromatic honey, such as heather honey
squeeze of lemon juice

Dissolve the yeast in 200ml of tepid water and set aside for 5 minutes to froth up. Sift the flour and sugar together into a bowl and make a well in the centre. When the yeast has dissolved, pour this into the well with another 200ml of water, the egg, the milk and a pinch of cinnamon. Mix well to make smooth, thin, batter-like dough.

Cover and set aside in a warm place for about an hour or until the dough has doubled in size. At this stage, you can knock back the dough and cover and refrigerate to use at another time, or use immediately.

To use it immediately, line a plate with kitchen paper and set aside. Heat the sunflower oil in a deep saucepan. To test when it is hot enough, carefully drop a teaspoon of the batter into the oil. If it starts to bubble and brown, the oil is ready.

Using a dessertspoon, gently drop spoonfuls of the batter into the oil – you can cook a couple of balls at a time. When the balls start to brown, turn them using long-handled tongs or a slotted spoon. When they are golden on all sides, remove to drain on the kitchen paper. Repeat until all the batter is cooked.

While the balls are cooling, heat the honey, lemon juice and another pinch of ground cinnamon in a small saucepan. Bring it to the boil and remove from the heat. Set all the dough balls on a serving plate and pour over the hot honey. Allow the honey mixture to soak in, pouring over a little more if necessary. Serve warm.

HONEY ROASTED SPICED NUTS

Serves 6–8

400g mixed nuts, such as cashew, almonds, pecan,
    walnuts and hazelnuts, shelled
1 garlic clove, crushed to a paste with salt
½ tbsp ground cumin
½ tbsp cumin seeds
1 tbsp smoked paprika
2 tsp ground coriander seeds
1 tsp mustard seeds
1 tsp ground cinnamon
pinch of chilli flakes or ¼ tsp ground chilli powder
90ml runny honey
2 tbsp olive oil

Preheat the oven to 170°C/325°F/Gas 3. In a large bowl, mix the nuts with the garlic paste and all the spices. Pour over the honey and oil and mix well.

Spread the nuts out on a large baking tray and set in the oven. Bake for 10 minutes, then stir the nuts well and return to the oven for a further 10 minutes. Remove and allow to cool before eating.

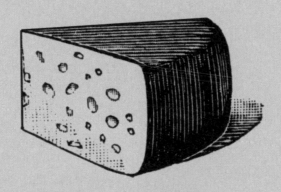

CHEESE

CHEESE
with RECIPES *by* GLYNN PURNELL

Soft and creamy, blue and salty, firm and crumbly – cheese comes in an astounding array of textures, strengths, shapes and even sizes. But true artisan cheese needs care and attention at every stage. People who make it their life's mission to bring us this amazing product lovingly craft each cheese. Over recent years there have been encouraging indications that good-quality British cheese is beginning to return to our shelves. So why does British cheese still need a revival?

Before World War II Britain had a thriving cheese making industry spread throughout the country. Prior to 1939 there were 3,500 cheese makers in the UK but when the War ended this number had shrunk to just a few hundred. The public taste had also changed and many of the wonderful regional varieties and methods of cheese-making were forgotten. When the time came to rediscover cheese, we started to rely on imports from France, Italy and elsewhere on the continent to satisfy our appetite.

Today, over half of the cheeses on sale in the UK are imported. And even our most popular cheese, cheddar, is just as likely to have been made in Poland or even Australia as it is to have been made in Britain. We've developed a taste for these imported cheeses and while you may be partial to a slice of Camembert, Danish Blue or Parmesan, have you tried Waterloo, Shropshire Blue or Berkswell? Our heritage cheeses are more delicious than any import and can be enjoyed in these recipes or simply generously heaped on a crisp cracker.

BAKED CHEDDAR CUSTARD
with COOKED *and* RAW BEETROOT SALAD

The reason I've chosen to do a baked cheddar custard is because it brings the best out of the sharpness of the cheddar. The top of it reminds me of cheese on toast, which brings back great memories of my childhood. *Glynn Purnell*

Serves 2

Custard
180g Cheddar cheese, grated
275ml double cream
½ tsp English Mustard
pinch of salt
½ tsp ginger powder
4 free range medium eggs

Dressing
50ml aged balsamic vinegar
200ml light olive or rapeseed oil
1 tsp icing sugar

Beetroot salad
½ candied beetroot, striped
½ orange beetroot, peeled
  and thinly sliced
½ red beetroot, peel and thinly slice
6 baby beetroot, cooked and
  split in half lengthways
1 small packet of cooked beetroot,
  diced
200g small red-vein sorrel leaves
100g watercress

Preheat the oven to 160°C/310°F/Gas 2½. Place 125g grated Cheddar cheese in a saucepan. Add the cream and the mustard and gently heat together to melt the cheese into the cream. Season with salt and ginger and pass through a sieve into a 10 x 20cm ovenproof dish. Sprinkle with the remaining grated cheese. Place in a roasting tin bain-marie, add boiling water to come halfway up the side of the dish and cook in the oven for 40 minutes. The custard should have a bit of a wobble to it when you take it out.

In a bowl, whisk together the balsamic vinegar, rapeseed oil and icing sugar and set aside. Place the raw beetroot and cooked baby beetroot in a bowl and pour over the balsamic dressing. Place the beetroot on a plate and top with the sorrel leaves and watercress. Serve with the warm baked cheese custard.

TAIL FILLET OF BEEF
with BLACK STICK BLUE BONBONS *with* SHALLOT PURÉE *and* ROCKET

This recipe is an interpretation of the classic pairing of blue cheese and fillet steak. I find this is a really delicate way of using cheese without overpowering the beef, and a great use of our fantastic British blues. The peppery flavour of the rocket really complements the flavour of the cheese. *Glynn Purnell*

Serves 2

Shallot purée
8 shallots, roughly diced
200g butter
50ml chicken stock

Fillet and jus
450g tail fillet on the bone,
   at room temperature
100ml red wine
300ml reduced beef stock
2 sprigs of thyme

Bonbons
200g plain flour
2 free range egg yolks, beaten
120g white breadcrumbs
100ml milk
50g Black Stick blue cheese
150g potatoes, boiled and mashed
10ml double cream
salt and pepper

rocket leaves, seasoned, to garnish

Preheat the oven to 240°C/475°F/Gas 9. Sweat the shallots with 50g butter, until translucent and not coloured. Add the chicken stock and simmer for one minute. Blend and pass through a fine sieve into a bowl. Set the tail fillet, bone-side down, in a roasting tray. Place into the oven and cook for 10–15 minutes. Remove and allow to rest.

For the bonbons, preheat the deep fat fryer with vegetable or sunflower oil to 170°C/325°F. If you don't have a deep fat fryer, use a medium-sized pan half full of oil. Place the flour and breadcrumbs in two separate bowls. Whisk the egg yolks with the milk and place in a third bowl. Crumble the blue cheese into the mashed potato. Add the cream and whip together to remove any lumps. Divide the mixture into 12 equal-sized balls.

Dip each ball first into the flour, then the egg wash and then the breadcrumbs. Repeat the process twice. Fry each ball for about 90 seconds, until they are golden. Do not let them get too hot in case they explode. Drain on kitchen paper and keep warm.

For the jus, place the roasting tray over a medium heat and add the remaining butter. Stir and add the red wine. Reduce to a syrup. Add the beef stock and thyme. Reduce to one-third of the original quantity and pass through a fine sieve into a bowl.

To serve, carve the fillet from the bone, and season with salt and pepper. Dress the plate with shallot purée. Arrange the meat on the plate with three bonbons and pour over some jus. Serve with the seasoned rocket alongside as a garnish.

VANILLA BAKED CHEESECAKE
with BLACKBERRIES *and*
BLACK PEPPER HONEYCOMB

Cheesecake is an obvious way to use cheese in a pudding. In this recipe, I have used a delicious West Yorkshire soft cheese with a very old-fashioned technique of baking the cheesecake. Serve it with some sharp juicy blackberries and crunchy honeycomb. *Glynn Purnell*

Serves 6

Cheesecake
200g digestive biscuits
55g butter
1 vanilla pod, seeds scraped out
500g full fat soft West Yorkshire cheese
3 free range eggs
juice of ½ a lemon
75ml double cream
55g plain flour
200g caster sugar

Blackberry purée
125g blackberries
10g caster sugar
splash of water

Black pepper honeycomb
35g honey
70g liquid glucose
200g caster sugar
20g bicarbonate of soda
freshly ground black pepper

You will need a 20cm springform cake tin, a silicone mat large enough to line a baking tray and a sugar thermometer. Preheat the oven to 140°C/275°F/Gas 1. Line the base of the springform cake tin with parchment paper. Blitz the biscuits in a food processor into crumbs. Melt butter in a saucepan and stir in the biscuit crumbs. Press the biscuit mixture into the bottom of the lined tin and place in the fridge to set.

Put the blackberries, sugar and water in a saucepan and simmer for about 10 minutes. Blitz in a blender and pass it through a fine sieve into a bowl. Allow to cool.

In a large bowl, stir the vanilla seeds into the cream cheese. Put the eggs, lemon juice and cream into a jug and whisk together. Add half of the egg mixture to the cream cheese and mix well. Stir the flour and sugar into the cream cheese mixture, and then stir in the rest of the egg mixture until smooth. Remove the cake tin from the fridge and pour the cheese mixture into it. Drizzle the cooled blackberry purée over the cheesecake mix and bake for 40 minutes.

To make the honeycomb, first place a silicone mat into a large baking tray and set aside. Put all of the ingredients apart from the bicarbonate of soda and black pepper into a large saucepan. Keeping track using a sugar thermometer, heat the mixture up to 150°C/300°F. Swiftly whisk in the bicarbonate of soda, (the volume of the mixture will more than double). Carefully pour onto the silicone mat, grind over black pepper and allow to cool. Break the honeycomb pieces over the top of the cheesecake and serve in slices.

TARTIFLETTE

Serves 6
1kg Desiree, Ratte or Charlotte potatoes, peeled
50g crème fraiche
1 garlic clove, crushed to a paste with salt
2 sprigs of thyme, leaves stripped and stems discarded
salt and pepper
500g Reblochon cheese or, for an English version, try Stinking Bishop

Preheat the oven to 220°C/425°F/Gas 7. Cook the potatoes in plenty of boiling, salted water until they are just soft and then drain them. When they are cool enough to handle, slice them into 1cm discs and place in a mixing bowl.

Add the crème fraiche, garlic paste and thyme leaves, season well and set aside. Slice the cheese into pieces about 1cm thick and set aside.

Place a layer of the potatoes into an ovenproof dish, and place some slices of cheese on top of the potato. Repeat this until all the potatoes and cheese are used up but finish with slices of cheese on top. Bake in the oven for 25–30 minutes or until the top has browned and the cheese has melted throughout. This is delicious served with cured meats and a green salad.

WATERCRESS, PEAR
and BLUE CHEESE SALAD

Serves 4

Dressing
1 garlic clove, crushed
   to a paste with salt
1 tbsp sherry vinegar
2 tbsp olive oil
salt and pepper

Salad
2 ripe Comice or Conference pears, peeled, cored and sliced
100g blue cheese, such as Beenleigh Blue or Black Sticks Creamy,
   cut into small pieces
50g walnuts, coarsely chopped
1 tbsp parsley, roughly chopped
100g watercress, rinsed and dried carefully

Make the dressing by placing the crushed garlic, sherry vinegar and olive oil in a bowl or jug. Whisk thoroughly, season with salt and pepper to taste and set aside.

Put the pears, cheese and walnuts in a roomy salad bowl and drizzle over a tablespoon or two of the dressing. Sprinkle over the parsley. Add the watercress and pour over the rest of the dressing. Toss together gently and serve immediately.

CHEESE FONDUE

Serves 4

1 loaf of good crusty bread, cut into chunks
1 garlic clove, crushed to a paste with salt
500ml dry cider
800g aged Gruyère or Lincolnshire Poacher cheese, grated
2 tbsp plain flour
pepper

You will need four fondue prongs.

Lightly grill the chunks of bread and set them aside until ready to serve.

Put the garlic paste and cider into a large, heavy-bottomed saucepan over a medium heat and bring to the boil. Place the cheese in a large bowl. Add the flour and toss together to coat.

When the cider is bubbling, add the cheese, a handful at a time, stirring well. Continue to do this until all the cheese is added and you have a smooth, melted mass. Do not let it boil or burn. Season well with the black pepper and serve, using the fondue prongs to dip the bread cubes into the cheese.

CHEESE SOUFFLÉ

Serves 6
20g unsalted butter, plus extra for greasing
50g Parmesan cheese, finely grated, plus extra for dusting
2 tbsp plain flour, heaped
250ml milk, warmed
salt and pepper
nutmeg, grated
150g Berkswell cheese, finely grated
4 free range eggs, separated

You will need a 0.5 litre soufflé dish.

Preheat the oven to 220°C/425°F/Gas 7. Place a baking tray on the middle shelf of the oven to heat. Butter a half-litre soufflé dish and then dust with some of the grated Parmesan cheese.

Melt the butter over a low heat in a saucepan then add the flour. Cook, stirring for a couple of minutes, until it just starts to brown. Gradually add the warmed milk, a little at a time, stirring well to prevent lumps. Once all the milk is added, continue to cook for 3–4 minutes, stirring all the time, until the sauce has thickened. Season well with salt and pepper and grate in some nutmeg. Pour the mixture into a large bowl and add the grated cheese. Mix well before whisking in the egg yolks and set aside.

In a separate bowl, whisk the egg whites. (It is important to make sure the bowl you whisk the whites in is dry, clean and free of grease. This will maximise the volume the egg whites whisk up to.) Whisk until the whites form stiff peaks then carefully fold them into the cheese mixture. Pour into the soufflé dish and bake for approximately 25 minutes or until it is well risen and golden on top. Serve immediately.

CHEDDAR *and* CARAWAY BISCUITS

Makes
about
15 biscuits

175g plain flour
pinch of ground chilli
½ tsp salt
125g unsalted butter, cut into cubes
200g mature British Cheddar, grated
2 tsp caraway seeds
1 free range egg, beaten

In a large bowl, sift the flour and chilli and add the salt. Chop in the cubes of butter until the mixture resembles coarse breadcrumbs. (You can do this in a food processor if you have one.)

Stir the grated cheese into the mixture and add the caraway seeds and the beaten egg. Mix lightly to form a soft dough. Bring the dough together and wrap in Cling film. Gently mould it into a thick sausage shape. If you are going to use it immediately, chill it in the freezer for 10 minutes. Otherwise, put it in the fridge and use it over the next couple of days as required.

To cook, preheat the oven to 190°C/375°F/Gas 5. Lightly grease a baking sheet and set it aside. Unwrap the dough and slice into discs about 1cm thick. Arrange them on the baking sheet and cook in the oven for about 20 minutes or until the biscuits are golden and crisp. Cool on a wire rack.

WELSH RAREBIT

Serves 6   25g butter
            25g plain flour
            1 tsp English mustard powder or 3 tsp English mustard
            150ml brown ale
            300g mature Cheddar cheese, such as Keen's, Montgomery's or Westcombe, grated
            3 tsp Worcestershire sauce
            6 slices of good white sandwich bread

Melt the butter in a saucepan. Add the flour and stir it in well. Continue stirring and cooking until the flour becomes nutty brown. Add the mustard and then the brown ale and stir well to get rid of any lumps.

When it is smooth, add the cheese and the Worcestershire sauce and cook until the cheese is melted, smooth and stretchy. Pour into a shallow tray to cool slightly.

To serve, lightly toast the bread and spread the cheese mixture over each slice. Grill for a couple of minutes or until bubbling and just brown.

LANCASHIRE CHEESE
and CHUTNEY SANDWICH

A reminder of how good simple things can be.

Makes 2
4 slices of good wholemeal or granary bread
30g butter, softened
2 tbsp green tomato chutney (see page 146)
200g Lancashire cheese, cut into slivers

Spread all four slices of bread with plenty of butter. Spread the chutney evenly over two of the slices and arrange layers of the slivered cheese over the chutney. Top with the other buttered pieces of bread. Cut in half to serve.

SUPPLIERS

Here are the details for farms, growers, shops and other suppliers of the ten great British ingredients used in this book.

BREAD

E5 Bakehouse
Arch 402, Mentmore Terrace,
London, E8 3PH
020 8986 3565

The School *of* Artisan Food
Lower Motor Yard, Welbeck,
Nottinghamshire, S80 3LR
www.schoolofartisanfood.org
01909 532171

Hambleton Bakery
Cottesmore Road, Exton,
Oakham, Rutland, LE15 8AN
www.hambletonbakery.co.uk
01572 812 995

CRAB

Billingsgate Fish Market
Trafalgar Way,
London, E14 5ST
www.billingsgate-market.org.uk
020 7987 1118

Sea Food *and* Eat It
www.seafoodandeatit.co.uk

Gee Whites
1 The High Street, Swanage,
Dorset, BH19 2LN
www.geewhites.co.uk
01929 42572

Barrafina
54 Frith Street,
London, W1D 4SL
www.barrafina.co.uk
020 7813 8016

Rex Goldsmith Fishmonger
10 Cale Street, Chelsea,
London, SW3 3QU
www.chelseafish.co.uk
020 7589 9432

POTATO

Luffness Mains
Aberlady, East Lothian,
EH32 0PZ
www.luffnessmains.com
01875 870 212

Science *and* Advice *for*
Scottish Agriculture
Roddinglaw Road,
Edinburgh, EH12 9FJ
www.sasa.gov.uk
0131 244 8890

Carroll's Heritage Potatoes
Tiptoe Farm,
Cornhill-on-Tweed,
Northumberland,
TD12 4XD
www.heritage-potatoes.co.uk
01890 882205

Peter Barratt's Garden Centre
Gosforth Park Avenue,
Newcastle upon Tyne, NE3 5EP
www.thegardencentregroup.co.uk
0191 236 7111

PORK

Meridian Meats Family Butchers
108 Eastgate, Town Centre,
Louth, Lincolnshire, LN11 9AA
www.meridianmeatsshop.co.uk
01506 603 357

Northfield Farm
Whissendine Lane, Cold Overton,
Oakham, Rutland, LE15 7QF
www.northfieldfarm.com
01664 474 271

Huntsham Court Farm
(Outstanding Rare Breed Meat)
Ross-on-Wye, Herts, HR9 6JN
www.huntsham.com
01600 890 296

CAULIFLOWER

Staples Cauliflower Farm
Marsh Farm, Boston,
Lincolnshire, PE22 9HE
www.staplesvegetables.co.uk
01205 872 900

Woodland's Farm
Kirton House, Boston,
Lincolnshire, PE20 1JD
www.woodlandsfarm.co.uk
01205 722 491

Doherty's Fruit *and*
Veg Farm Shop
Four Seasons Garden Centre,
Lincolnshire, NG34 8NY
01529 304 970

Sleaford Market
Sleaford, Lincolnshire
01529 301 854

Yotam Ottolenghi
www.ottolenghi.co.uk

Able *and* Cole
16 Waterside Way,
London, SW17 0HB
www.abelandcole.co.uk
020 8944 3780

Riverford Organic Vegetables
Buckfastleigh, Devon,
TQ11 0JU
www.riverford.co.uk
01803 762 059

MUTTON

Welsh Farm Organics
Tyn Y Fron, Mochdre,
Powys, SY16 4JW
www.welshfarmorganics.org.uk
01686 627979

Abergavenny Food Festival
Market St, Abergavenny,
Gwent, NP7 5XZ
*www.abergavennyfood
festival.com*
01873 851 643

Café Caribbean Warren
Taj Stores, 112 Brick Lane,
Spitalfields, London, E1 6RL
020 7377 6443

Sheepdrove Organic Farm
Sheepdrove Road, Lambourn,
Berkshire, RG17 7UU
www.sheepdrove.com
01488 674747

Café Spice Namasté
16 Prescot Street, London,
E1 8AZ
www.cafespice.co.uk
020 7488 9242

Moens Butchers
24 The Pavement, Clapham
Common, London, SW4 0JA
www.moen.co.uk
020 7622 1624

Elan Valley Mutton
www.elanvalleymutton.co.uk
01597 811240

The Blackface Meat Company
Weatherall Foods Limited,
Crochmore House, Irongray,
Dumfries, DG2 9SF
www.blackface.co.uk
01387 730 326

TOMATO

New Covent Garden Market
London, SW8 5BH
www.newcoventgardenmarket.com
020 7720 2211

Eric Wall Limited
Pollards Nursery, Barnham,
Bognor Regis, PO22 0AF
01243 555 598

Guy & Wright
The Nurseries, Green Tye,
Hertfordshire, SG10 6JJ
www.guyandwright.com
01279 842444

Audley End House *and* Gardens
Saffron Walden, CB11 4JF
01799 522148

Brighton *and* Hove
Grow Your Neighbour's Own
Drove Road, Portslade,
Brighton, BN41 2PA
*www.beachstone.co.uk/
growyourneighboursown/*
01273 431 714

Temptation Café
56 Gardner Street,
Brighton, BN1 1UN
01273 673 045

Isle of Wight Tomatoes
Wight Salads, Nursery Main
Road, Isle of Wight, PO30 3AR
www.thetomatostall.co.uk
01983 866 907

APPLE

Brogdale Farm *and*
National Fruit Collection
Brogdale Road, Faversham,
Kent, ME13 8XZ
www.brogdalecollections.co.uk
01795 536250

Rough Old Wife Cider
Hawkins Rough Orchard,
Long Hill, Canterbury,
Kent, CT4 8BN
www.rougholdwife.com
01227 732414

Little Sharsted Farm
Doddington, Sittingbourne,
Kent, ME9 0JT
01795 886263

Chegworth Valley
Water Lane Farm, Chegworth,
Harrietsham, Kent, ME17 1DE
www.chegworthvalley.com
01622 859272

New Ash Green Woodland
Group
www.nagwoodlands.btck.co.uk

HONEY

The Hive Honey Shop
93 Northcote Road, London,
SW11 6PL
www.thehivehoneyshop.co.uk
020 7924 6233

Oakfield Honey Farm
West Street, Steeple Claydon,
Buckinghamshire, MK18 2LI
01296 730794

Rowse Honey
The Beehive, Rowse Honey
Limited, Moreton Avenue,
Wallingford, Oxfordshire
OX10 9DE
www.rowsehoney.co.uk
0800 954 8089

Urban Bees
www.urbanbees.co.uk
07930 337907

Chelsea Physic Gardens
66 Royal Hospital Road,
London, SW3 4HS
www.chelseaphysicgarden.co.uk

CHEESE

Butlers Farmhouse Cheeses
Wilson Fields Farm,
Inglewhite, Preston,
Lancashire, PR3 2LH
www.butlerscheeses.co.uk

Montgomery's Cheddar
Manor Farm, North Cadbury,
Yeovill, Somerset,
BA22 7DW
*www.farmhousecheesemakers.
com/cheesemakers/
montgomery_s_cheddar*
01963 440243

Frome Farmer's Market
Market Yard, Frome,
Somerset, BA11 1BE
*www.somersetfarmersmarkets.
co.uk/markets/frome*
01373 812757

Neal's Yard Diary
6 Park Street, London, SE1 9AB
www.nealsyarddairy.co.uk
020 7367 0799

Moorlands Cheesemakers
South Street, Castle Cary,
Somerset, BA7 7ES
www.cheesemaking.co.uk
01963 350634

Leagram Organic Dairy
High Head Farm Buildings,
Green Lane, Chipping
Near Preston, Lancashire,
PR3 2TQ
www.leagromorganicdiary.co.uk
01995 61532

Mrs Kirkham's
Beesley Farm, Goosnargh,
Preston, Lancashire, PR32FL
www.mrskirkhams.com
01772 865335

Lincolnshire Poacher Cheese
F.W. Read & Sons Limited,
Ulceby Grange, Alford,
Licolnshire, LN13 0HE
*www.lincolnshirepoacher
cheese.com*
01507 466 987

RECIPE LIST

INDEX

ACKNOWLEDGEMENTS

Outline Productions is the company behind the concept of the *Great British Food Revival* and produced the TV series on which the book is based. I'd like to thank Claire Urquhart for helping me develop this idea and Lindsay Bradbury at the BBC for seeing its potential and helping to get it commissioned for BBC2. The idea would never have come to life if it wasn't for the chefs' participation and I would like to thank them for the enthusiasm and passion they brought to the series. Huge thanks to the Outline production team as they did such a fantastic job. Series Producer Philip J. Smith has delivered a show with real content and ambition. Producers Marc Beers and Philippa Murphy did an excellent job and they were very well assisted by Sam Knowles and George Hughes. The research team of Sam Palmer, Alice Binks and Kate Williams found some great stories and excellent contributors. Thanks also to our brilliant support team of Barbara Browne, Rainier Chapman and Carolyn Pearson, and to Diana Hunter who gave invaluable advice throughout. Thanks to Sarah Myland for shooting so beautifully and to her sound recordist James Nightingale. Bethany Heald, Faenia Moore and Georgia May ran a tight kitchen and thanks to the kitchen runners Harry Kaufman, Melanie Prescott and Alex Howard. Our off-line editors Dan Smith, Matthew Dodd-Noble and Martin Strike did a superb job and thanks to Edit producer Sophie Seiden and Edit assistant Abbi Issac who worked long and hard to ensure the edits ran as smoothly as possible. Thanks must also go to Halo post production facility, to Sharon Spencer and Patrick Brazier at the Station for the graphics and to Dan McGrath and Josh Philips for the title music. At Orion, I would like to thank Lisa Milton and Amanda Harris for commissioning the book and for their enormous enthusiasm for the project. Also to Andrew Hayes-Watkins for his stunning photography and to Blanche Vaughan for her delicious recipes. Thanks also to the Orion team of Nicola Crossley, Natasha Webber, Kate Barr and Clare Hennessy.

Lastly I'd like to thank my family for all their support. They have endured food shopping trips with me recently which have become more like treasure hunts as I seek out fantastic British seasonal produce. This project has changed my buying and eating habits and I hope this book will encourage you to review yours.

Bridget Boseley *Executive Producer, Outline Productions*